THE TECHNICAL MANAGER'S SURVIVAL GUIDES

TEAM BUILDING

By Marcus Goncalves

ASME Press ♦ **New York**

Library of Congress Cataloging-in-Publication Data

Goncalves, Marcus.
The technical manager's survival guides team building / by Marcus Goncalves.
p. cm.
Includes bibliographical references.
ISBN 0-7918-0251-5
1. Teams in the workplace. 2. Organizational effectiveness. I. Title.

HD66.G65 2006
658.4'022--dc22

2006022107

Dedication

To my forever beautiful wife Carla, my son and friend Samir, and especially, in memory of my princess and daughter Andrea, and my young prince Joshua, who passed away during the writing of this book. These are the real treasures of my life.

To God be the glory.

Marcus Goncalves

Preface

Making teams more productive is a constant issue for most managers. Productivity is, of course, the essence of what makes businesses competitive, but it is particularly important in times of economic slowdown such as the one we are currently experiencing.

A common pitfall seen in business organizations is the confusion between a "group" and a "team." With "team" being a buzzword in today's business world, we often think that any work in which various people work together is, by definition, a team. This is a gross error. We have always worked as a group. A restaurant, for example, is a group in which there is a general manager, cooks, waiters and waitresses, cleaning people, and so on. Each person performs specific tasks given to him or her by management, and each person is evaluated according to how well he or she has done the task at hand. They work as a group, but not as a team.

In *Team Building*, you will be able to understand how a team is not collective, but as opposed to a group, decisions are shared, the rules are internally established, and the rewards (or punishments) are shared by all. In my consulting experience I have noticed a trend across the industry in actively pushing team-building as a strategy to force people to cooperate with one another, thus getting rid of the usual internal fighting that costs companies plenty. My hope is that this book will provide you with an overview of what teams are and what they are not, as well as some strategies and activities for building teams.

This book is not, however, intended to comprehensively cover the subject. There is a lot of resources available out there and the bibliography may help you in expanding your knowledge on the topic. The idea of this book is to provide you with a good overview on the topic. The book also should serve as a resource companion for those professionals attempting the Engineering Management Certificate International (EMCI) offered by the American Society of Mechanical Engineers (ASME). But, of course, this book can be of great use to any business professionals seeking to develop effective and high performance teams.

The book is broken up into two sections, one providing the fundamentals of team building and the second one providing additional perspectives and tools for developing teams. Here it is an overview of the book:

Chapter 1, *Fundamentals of Team Building: Challenges and Rewards*, provides an overview of team building, its challenges, rewards, as well as a differentiation between teams and other groups of professionals. Chapter 2, *Working as a Team*, provides an insight on the advantages of having an organization investing on team building and working as such. Chapter 3, *Fostering Culture Change*, conveys the importance of preparing organizations and team change before they have to, by demonstrating how changes occur and how it impacts team performance if it is not prepared to deal with it. Chapter 4, *Going Beyond Team Building: The*

Art of Enchanting, shows how important it is for team leaders to be able to inspire their teams, and how managing and leading is not the same, and that a team, to be effective needs both. Chapter 5, *Moving the Cheese: Preparing Teams for Change*, picks up where chapter 3 left by bringing a pragmatic approach to change management and how high performance teams can capitalize on it. Chapter 6, *Mastering Team Management*, is the last chapter of section one, providing information how to effective lean and manage the development and performance of teams.

The second section of this book attempts to enhance the quality of teams being built by alerting to the importance of *team diversity* in chapter 7; the development of *self-directed and self-managed teams*, as well as the advantages and disadvantages of each team structure in chapter 8; the need for building and managing *virtual teams* in chapter 9; and finally, chapter 10 provides some *team building activities* to get you started.

Who Should Read This Book

This book is primarily designed for those who have or will be assigned team building and management responsibilities; for project and team managers, project and team leaders or anyone performing in those roles or soon to be performing in those roles.

Acknowledgment

I have been incubating this book in my mind for quite some time. A lot of it is a result of my own consulting work, but the Project Management Institute (PMI) resources also played a major role in it; so did the many professionals I work with every day.

To thank every single one of them here would be impossible, so if I miss some of their names, please forgive me. I would like to start thanking Mary Grace Stefanchik, the editor at the American Society of Mechanical Engineers, for not only inviting me to write this book, but especially for her patience with me and my busy schedule, to professor Vijay Kanabar, at Boston University for his great friendship, and excellent insights in project management, in which he is a great professionals and PMP. My gratitude also goes to Pamela Campagna, president of Blue Sage Consulting, for her excellent insights, and for picking up after me while I was busy writing this book; Newton Scavone, director of Human Resources at International Paper of Brazil, for his expert feedbacks prior to the conclusion of these writings; Michael Useem, at the Wharton School of Management, author of Leading Up, for his contribution and many valuable insights; Dorothy Leonard, from Harvard Business School, author of the book Wellspring of Knowledge, for her insightful feedbacks and permission to use some of her references; professor Kip Becker, Ph.D., Chairman, Department of Administrative Sciences at Boston University; and professor Marylee Rambaud, at Boston University School of Education, for constant support, from editing notes, to helping me set my priorities straight!

I would also like to express my appreciation to many corporate leaders that shared their views and experiences with me about team building, project and operations management. My special thanks go to the following leaders: Kerri Apple, VP of Marketing at bTrade; Gregory Baletsa, president of Astra Zeneca; Mark Lukoviski, of Microsoft; Carla Dimond, Sun Microsystems; Donald Eastlake III, from Motorola; Larry Miller, from PPL Montana; James Willey, of Covanta Energy of the Philippines, Luis Ferro, SAP Brazil; Mark Payne, of International Paper in U.S.; David Mellor, from Oracle; Susan Osterfelt, from Bank of America; and Michael Tinkleman, Ph.D., director of research at ASME in Washington, D.C. for all his support.

Many thanks also go to my spiritual leader at the Boston Church of Christ, Ken Ostrowski, for his continuous support and friendship. Last but not least, my deepest gratitude to my wife Carla, sons Samir and Josh (in memory), and my princess Andrea (in memory), for their unconditional support during the many hours it took to write this book. I could not forget Ninigapa (in memory of Paganini, previous bird), my parakeet, and Gus, the dog!

Glory be to God!

Table of Contents

Chapter 1 Fundamentals of Team Building: Challenges and Rewards

Unless teams are prepared to take reasonable risks, they are unlikely to develop independence and the ability to innovate.

Many studies show professionals benefit from working cooperatively. However, rarely published in literature are guidelines to help team builders effectively develop teams in the organization. There are a lot of how-to and team-building activities books, but not many discussing the fundamentals of team building. In my consulting experience I always make sure to explain to our clients how to create a positive learning experience by explaining team dynamics, and by using team contracts and team-building activities. We also share templates for evaluating team projects. I believe any team leader can benefit from such strategy.

Team builders should view themselves not only as professionals and subject matter experts in their particular fields, but also as educators. As such, their job is to prepare professionals for excellence with the task at hand, collaboration among their peers, and business success. These varied professional paths require that team members have training in communication and interpersonal skills, team planning, team decision-making processes, and leadership skills. Many organizations have a slew of courses available and promoted by human resources (Motorola has its own university) courses built into their curriculum to help their people develop communication skills, which is key in any successful team interaction. However, based on my 19 years of experience in this area, professional training in understanding team planning, decision making, and team dynamics is rudimentary compared to the explicit business (making money!) instruction professionals receive throughout their academic formation.

How do organizations use the diverse skills brought to a project by different members of a team? What level of planning is necessary at the outset, and how much communication among team members is needed to keep a project running smoothly? Professionals working in teams (or aspiring to build one!) need to know how to work effectively in teams, but the skills and processes required for effective team work, which are typical in business and communication courses, are usually not part of the science curriculum[1]. We use teamwork in our organizations because the benefits of cooperative work are numerous and varied, including an increased understanding of content, improved ability to explain concepts to peers, and improved business effectiveness.

We tend to place professionals in groups and then leave them on their own without instructions as to what they could expect from each other, what normal team behavior might resemble or how to work through challenging team dynamics. Yet we call this group of people a team! Our approach tends to be reactive rather than proactive, especially in more technical fields, such as engineers like us, who are very focused on what we do best and like to do well. When peers come to us about problems with team members, typically, our response tends to be little more than "work it out among yourselves." Our subsequent professional development activities, however, show us that this response is not effective in building teams.

This chapter focuses on the fundamentals of team building, as well as the logistics team leaders face when team members work together on a project. When we think of engineering-oriented projects in particular, all of these projects tend to be technical in nature, with not much room for team building activities (unless HR demands it!). So, what is involved in building teams?

The Four Development Phases of a Team

You can't do it alone! Building and maintaining teams in the workplace is crucial to any job these days. Developing teams and individual team members is key to help professionals develop the necessary skills and abilities for effective and motivating staff management and problem solving. Although we will be discussing this topic in much more detail in chapter 6, building a team may be viewed in five distinct phases, as depicted in figure 1.1:

- The "forming" phase is when the team is in reality still a collection of individuals dealing with procedural issues and the atmosphere is often artificially polite. Enthusiasm for and commitment to the new team is high but competence is low.

- The "storming" phase is when the team members begin to experiment and flex their muscles. Relationships become stormier both between members and between the team and other groups, and members question outside influences such as set procedures. As the team struggles to find the best way to work together, members may experience a temporary lapse in commitment.

- The "norming" phase is where the team is beginning to achieve its potential. It has developed its own way of working that is producing results.

- The "performing" phase is where the team is fully mature and effective. It deals with change in an open and flexible way, constantly challenges itself but avoids damaging conflicts. Development of team members is a high priority.

---

[1] See Brown, N.W 2000. *Creating high-performance classroom teams.* New York: Falmer Press.

- The "adjourning" phase is when the team is dispersed. Too often this phase is excluded from the set, but this is an important phase, as team members should share lessons learned, be reassigned and have a chance of synthesize their experience while still in the team.

See Figure 1.1 – The five phases of team building

Teams are unlikely to develop their potential without a struggle. They can get stuck in the early stages if members are too polite and not prepared to challenge the status quo. Teams may also become complacent after they reach an acceptable level of performance. If teams stagnate or encounter problems that they cannot overcome from their own resources, they will need help from management. This may include clarifying objectives, providing additional resources, training and team building exercises.

More on Forming a Team

There are three common ways of determining team composition: random, professional or function-directed, and team leader-directed. Many organizations tend to use random and function-directed team determination, but have not tried the team leader-directed method. I have seen many organizations randomly assigning professionals to teams because it reflects real-life situations; you do not often get to pick whom you work with on committees or assignments. Examples of how organizations have ensured randomness include having professionals draw playing cards or numbers out of a hat. Random team formation also avoids the perception that team leaders treat team members unequally. Although team members often express apprehension about this form of team determination, these teams often work out very well; I have had team members who first met working on a chemical lab project become inseparable friends for the rest of the project and beyond.

Occasionally, team leaders allow team members to self-select team members. Most team members seem to prefer this method, saying that they know whom they can or cannot work with, that they may have similar professional backgrounds, and that they know how seriously they are taking the project. One drawback I see in this process is that these teams are more likely to support a "free rider," a friend let off the hook without contributing to the team[2]. Another drawback I see is that team members who do not know anyone in the team can feel left out.

It is useful for team building to occur within the very early stage of a project. This allows the team to begin functioning as a team during the team-building activities and to work together on all aspects of the project: creating a team contract, forming workgroups, reviewing project scope and specifications, collecting data, and analyzing and presenting the results.

[2] See Michaelsen, L.K., A. Knight, and L. Fink. 2002. *Team-based learning: A transformative use of small groups.* West Port, CT: Greenwood Publishing Group.

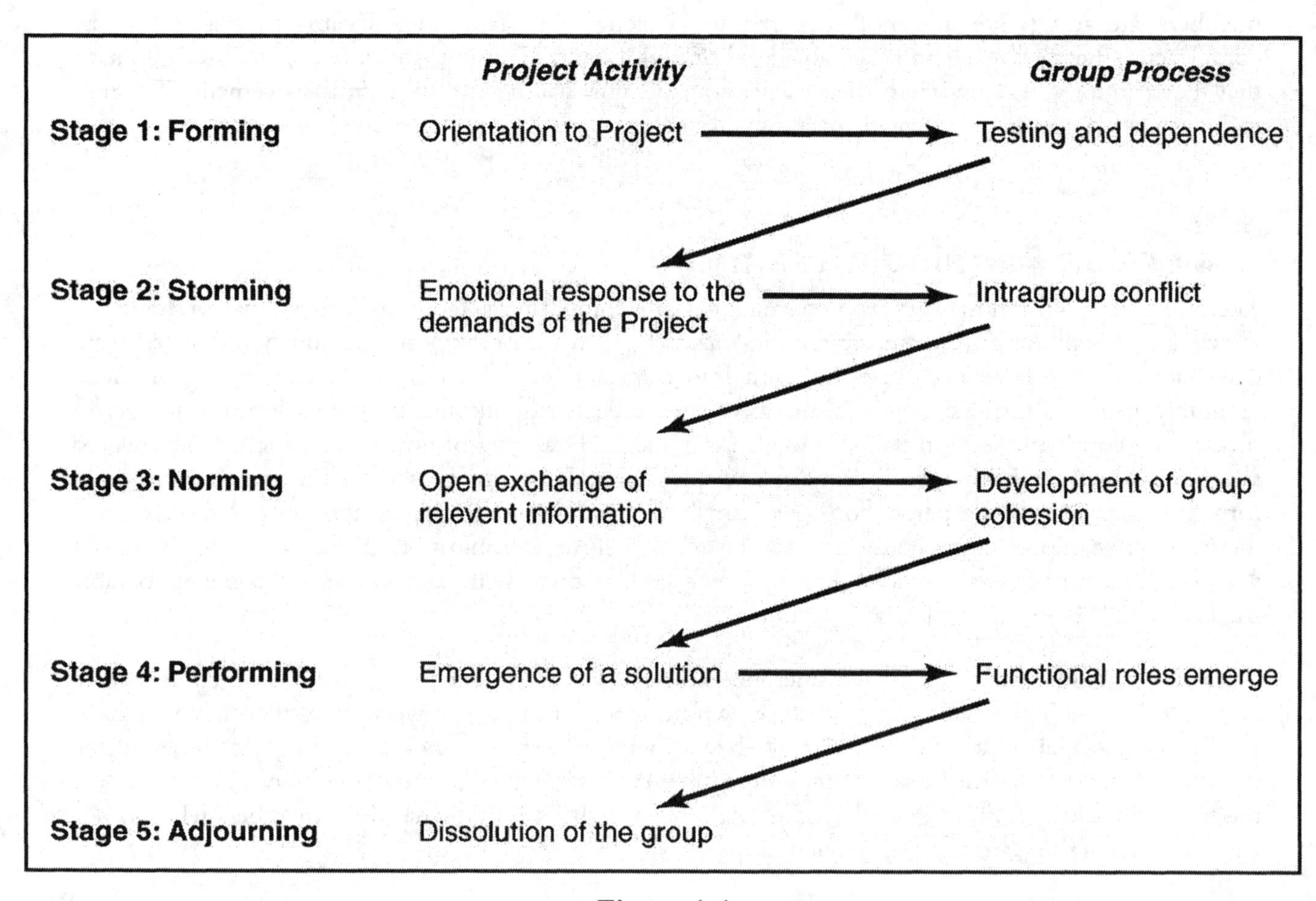
Project Activity
Group Process
Stage 1: Forming
Orientation to Project
Testing and dependence
Stage 2: Storming
Emotional response to the demands of the Project
Intragroup conflict
Stage 3: Norming
Open exchange of relevent information
Development of group cohesion
Stage 4: Performing
Emergence of a solution
Functional roles emerge
Stage 5: Adjourning
Dissolution of the group

Figure 1.1

Team Member's Self-Regulation

Team members' self-regulation is necessary if teamwork is to be achieved. Teams will always be subject to management direction of some degree or another and it is important that the boundaries of their authority are understood from early stages. Nevertheless research indicates that self-regulation tends to be lacking in those teams that are not performing to their full potential.

It is important to remember, however, that self-regulation will not happen automatically but must be developed. The task of team leaders when building their teams is to oversee the development of teams and provide the necessary support and training. There will also be a need for team leaders to accept that mistakes will be made as teams are given more responsibility. The emphasis should be on learning from mistakes rather than establishing blame. Unless teams are prepared to take reasonable risks, they are unlikely to develop independence and the ability to innovate.

Self-regulation often begins within the team as members decide on the order in which tasks should be tackled and their distribution among members. As teams develop, they can take on more responsibility for quality, production methods, hours and times of work and the selection of, or discipline of, team members. Mature teams may also manage their own relationships with other teams and take on responsibility for dealing with the wider organization in such matters as the provision of finance and resources.

There are three cyclical phases that seem to emerge in the acquisition of self-regulation skills, as depicted in figure 1.2:

- Phase 1, the forethought/pre-action - This phase precedes the actual performance; sets the stage for action; maps out the tasks to minimize the unknown; and helps to develop a positive mindset. Realistic expectations can make the task more appealing. Goals must be set as specific outcomes, arranged in order from short-term to long-term. We have to ask team members to consider the following:

    - When will they start?
    - Where will they do the work?
    - How will they get started?
    - What conditions will help or hinder their activities are a part of this phase?

  For instance, Gus must be helped to think about his project initiation tasks and reflect on what he can do to be more successful when he goes out. Is there a better time or place to do his stuff? Should he begin it in the morning with his friend Ninigapa, who are is doing better than he is in holding the branch? Should he plan to spend at least five minutes on a problem before giving up the carrots and moving on? Should he have a Ninigapa standing by to help either in person or on the phone (a supporting peer)?

- Phase 2, performance control - This phase involves processes during learning and the active attempt to utilize specific strategies to help a team members become more successful. You should ask team members the following:

- Are the team members accomplishing what they hoped to do?
  - Are they being distracted?
  - Is the project taking more time than they thought?
  - Under what conditions do they accomplish the most?
  - What questions can they ask themselves while they are working?

  How can team members encourage themselves to keep working (including self-talk—come on, get your work done so you can take some time off!)? For instance, Gus has to consider his performance in project scheduling as opposed to other areas of the project. When frustration increases, should Gus stop and take a break? Should he do his work right away or should he put it off until later, when he is more inspired? He is supposed to be using and considering the success or failure of some of the strategies he has thought about in phase 1.

- Phase 3, Self-reflection - This phase involves reflection after the performance, a self-evaluation of outcomes compared to goals. You have to ask team members to consider the following:
  - Did they accomplish what they planned to do?
  - Were they distracted and how did they get back to work?
  - Did they plan enough time or did they need more time than they thought?
  - Under what conditions did they accomplish the most work?

  For instance, Gus might ask, "What did I do differently?" "Did it work?" Was a change in time or work habits effective at solving more project problems? Did calling a team member who had experience in that same area of work makes a difference? Did setting a minimum time frame help? Did praising oneself aloud during successful times have a positive impact? (All right, I did it!! Yes, I solved that problem!!)

See Figure 1.2 – The three cyclical phases in the team member's acquisition of self-regulation skills

The development of good self-regulation usually involves the following:

- Self-observation - systematically monitoring own performance; keeping records is a big part of this!!
- Self-judgment - systematically comparing performance with a standard or goal (e.g., re-examining answers; checking procedures; rating answers in relation to answer sheet, another person's)

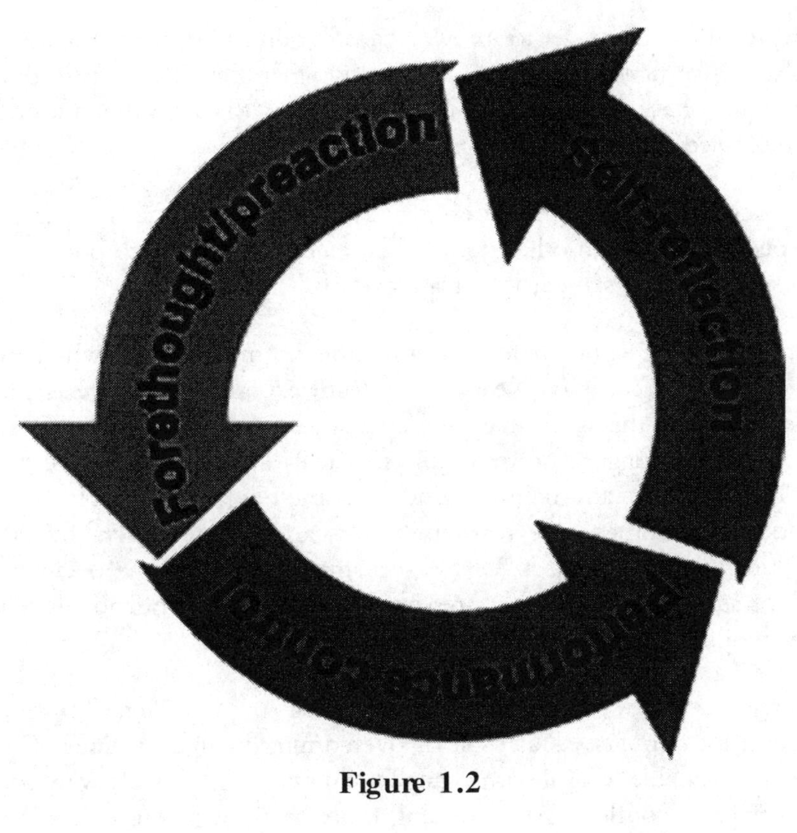
Forethought/preaction
Self-reflection
Performance control

Figure 1.2

- Self-reaction - engage in personal processes (i.e., goal-setting; meta-cognitive planning; behavioral outcomes); self-administering praise or criticism; rehearsing, memorizing; proximal goal setting; structuring environment (e.g. change project task's difficulty; change the project setting, the immediate physical environment; create a working area); asking for help, etc.

Work organization theorists have described developmental models for teams. These should not be used as prescriptions but can aid understanding, particularly if a team does not seem to be developing.

Understanding Team Dynamics

Every team needs to know from the beginning that there are phases of team performance. These phases, discussed earlier (forming, storming, norming, performing and adjourning), are very important to the development of a solid and high-performance team.

In the forming stage, team members get to know each other and a team contract is agreed upon. Team members begin to share information about themselves and what they expect from the project. Make sure to spend some time in this phase until everyone is comfortable with each other and the consistency of the team. More will be discussed on this aspect later, in chapter 6.

The norming phase occurs when team members strive to meet each other's expectations. Even if team members work independently of each other during this stage, trust begins to build as each team member completes tasks on time and at the standard the team expects.

The storming phase may occur either before or after the norming phase, when one or more of the members do not live up to the contract. Nearly every team experiences this phase, and it is critical that team members understand that this is normal. The intensity and duration varies from team to team and project to project. Events that trigger a storming phase usually involves the failure of a team member to meet a given deadline or when a team member hands in something that is at a lower standard than other team members' work. Other times, one team member can alienate others by taking on too much responsibility or by redefining the project. I have seen the storming phase occur immediately prior to important deadlines, or as a result of outside pressures, especially with individuals who tend to be more emotional about their work.

The performing phase occurs when the team works past the conflict. At this point, the team's performance becomes a lot stronger, as a result of overcoming their difficulties. The team is now fully mature and effective. It is capable to deal with change in an open and flexible way, constantly challenging itself, but avoiding damaging conflicts. At this point, more than ever before, the development of team members is a high priority.

The idea of teamwork as the most appropriate form of work organization for shop-floor production or the delivery of services assumes the long-term contribution of teams. It would be unrealistic to expect a team's “performing” phase to continue indefinitely and consequently most teams enter the fifth phase, adjourning. Some teams may be terminated at this stage, however, others will enter a phase of renewal, or “reforming” which will probably involve beginning the development cycle again.

Team Contracts

You should conduct a team-building activity before you talk about the team's contract. In creating a contract, you should ask team members to list all the tasks they think will be associated with carrying out the project. Each team creates a contract that addresses the tasks, how important (on a scale of 1-10) each task is, and what deadline should be set for each task. As the team lists the tasks, team members choose which tasks they will handle.

The team contract also decides how conflicts are managed. Would all team members be part of the conversation? Would the conversation be face to face? Having team members think through how they will handle conflict before it occurs is a powerful way for teams to learn about conflict resolution. Figure 1.3 lists some attitudes towards conflict resolution and avoidance.

See Figure 1.3 – Alternatives for resolving conflicts

Team-Building Activities

In its early stages, it is very important that team builders try to pit teams against each other on small projects, using some simple activities that take less than 15 minutes to complete. The objective is to build team spirit. You can use a variety of activities to capitalize on multiple intelligences and to help teams work through problems.

If you know teams are experiencing conflict in their project, you can choose an activity that will help diffuse conflict among team members (usually something silly). If you notice that a specific team member has taken on a more aggressive role in their team, you can choose an activity that evens out individual contributions to the team score. If you see that one team member is being excluded from team conversations, you can choose an activity that gives individual members different information.

The communication and coordination of all that information is critical to the successful completion of the task. You can, for example, get your team to play Pictionary and complete mind puzzles. You can give math problems and have team members compete physically, throwing tennis balls into targets at varying points in the landscape. You can also play a version of the newlywed game, asking questions like, "How many pets will your partner say he has?"

Case Study: How Not to Build a Team, or the Blame Game

In any engineering organization, things go wrong. Product is shipped that doesn't meet customer expectations. Defects, perhaps severe ones, are missed in testing and discovered in the field. Documentation and manuals contains mistakes. The list goes on and on.

There are two possible responses to such a crisis. Some project managers will ask: "What can we change to make sure this kind of problem doesn't reoccur?" Other project managers will ask: "Who was responsible for this mistake?" They will begin to play the Blame Game.

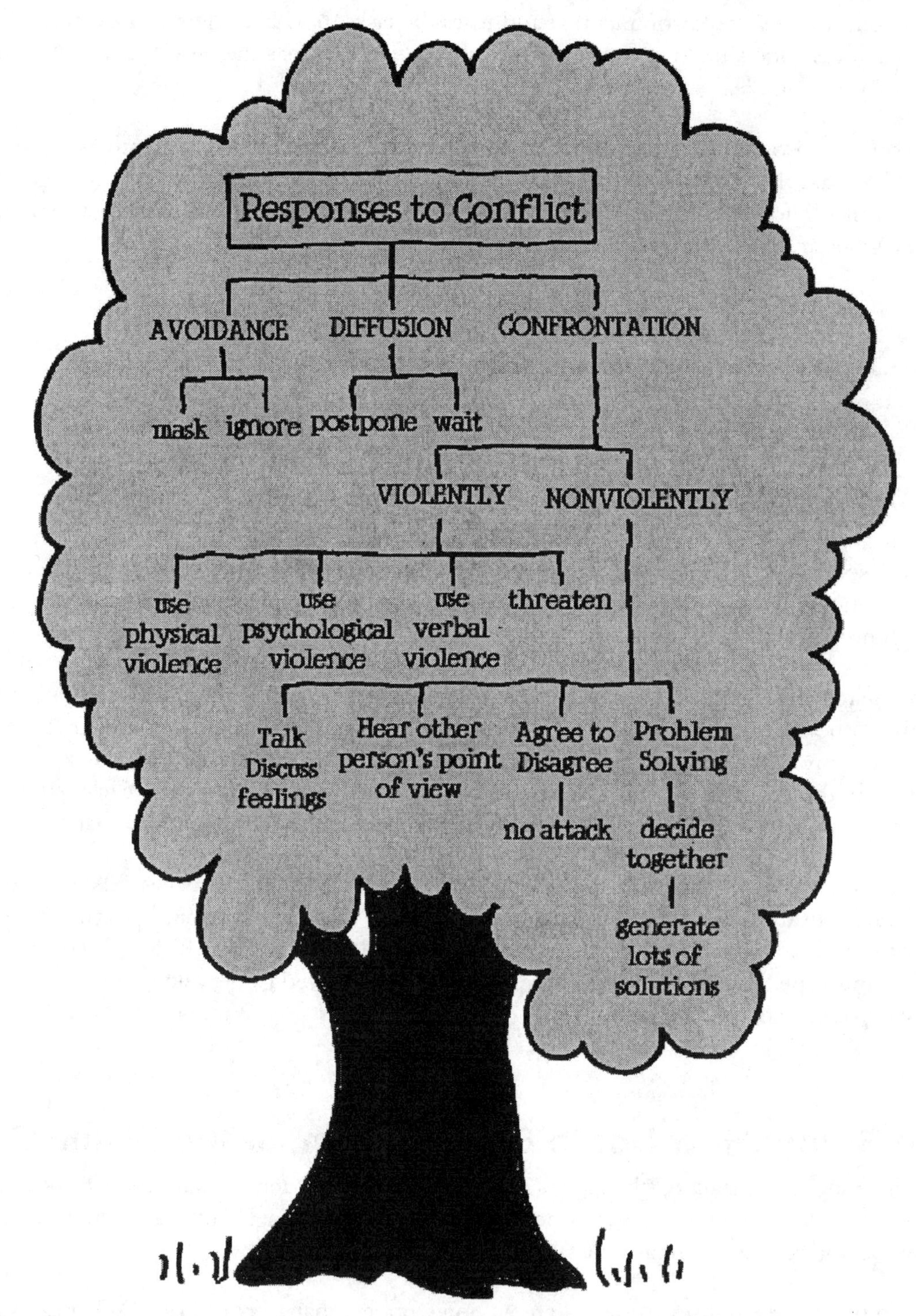
Responses to Conflict
AVOIDANCE
DIFFUSION
CONFRONTATION
mask
ignore
postpone
wait
VIOLENTLY
NONVIOLENTLY
use physical violence
use psychological violence
use verbal violence
threaten
Talk Discuss feelings
Hear other person's point of view
Agree to Disagree
Problem Solving
no attack
decide together
generate lots of solutions

Figure 1.4

A Game with No Winners, Only Losers

The Blame Game is a fun game to play. It allows a team leader to find some outlet for everyone's anger and frustration. It provides hours of entertaining conversation, and redirects uncomfortable responsibility in another direction.

The only real problem with the Blame Game is that it is impossible for anyone to ever win. Temporary victories are possible. When the CEO asks for an explanation of a screw-up, it's comforting to point the finger at one of the engineers and say: "He did it!"

Unfortunately, that solves nothing. The mistake still has to be corrected, the customer is still unhappy, and now the engineer who made the mistake is unhappy too. The mistake is just as likely to happen all over again next time.

If the CEO has the brains of an oyster, the Blame Game won't work for long. Very soon the realization will come: this project manager can't deliver the goods.

Who Makes Mistakes Anyway?

Some engineers make very few mistakes. These are the engineers who do as little as possible. They decline to rock the boat. They certainly will never try to improve anything. They follow the herd, well to the rear. Since they never initiate, they can never be blamed. These engineers look forward to their paycheck and don't spend much time worrying about the quality of the product. After all, it's not their problem.

Other engineers like to make things better. They are always looking to improve the product, and produce it more cheaply. These engineers are constantly making decisions. They are the ones on the cutting edge of progress. Nothing but the best is good enough for them. These are the engineers who make the most mistakes.

They are also the engineers who are responsible for all the progress. In an organization that plays the Blame Game, these engineers are the biggest losers.

What Would Captain Kirk Do in a Situation Like This?

As an old trekkie I'm quite familiar with the adventures of Captain Kirk and his diverse crew. While there are plenty of things that he can be criticized for, like his ceaseless violations of the Federation Prime Directive, there was one thing that Kirk knew how to do well: he knew how to accept responsibility.

In how many episodes did we hear Kirk explain that the captain is responsible for the actions of his crew? When things went wrong on the Starship Enterprise, Kirk never turned to Spock and asked: "who screwed up this time?" He instantly turned his full attention on resolving the current crises, and took full responsibility for any damage. There's a good lesson there for project managers.

Who Is Really To Blame?

When a mistake is made by anyone on the team, it is far more accurate to blame the project manager. After all, the project manager is supposed to understand that people are imperfect. He or she is supposed to devise processes and systems to catch mistakes. If that's not the job of a project manager, what is?

Since it's the project manager's job to establish the work process, it's also his or her responsibility. If a defect works its way through the process, then the process is broken and needs to be fixed. If instead of trying to fix it, the project manager decides to play the Blame Game, the process will remain broken. Look for more defects in the next release.

Engineers very quickly learn to cope with the Blame Game. After all, they are good at solving problems. There are two solutions to the Blame Game problem, from an engineer's point of view. Either stop trying to improve anything, or find another job. The second solution is usually the best one.

Here's a Dollar, Go Buy a Clue

Nothing destroys respect for a project manager faster than the Blame Game. It might only take one round of play to completely lose the respect of everyone on your team. Only a few more rounds are required to lose the respect of upper management as well.

Next time a defect is discovered in your product, instead of blaming the engineer responsible, go out and buy a book or two about the process of professional engineering. Spend some time working on test plans. Set up a work review process to catch future mistakes. Do something useful.

Most importantly, take responsibility. Apologize to the entire team for the process defect that caused the product defect. Pull a Captain Kirk.

You'll find that you not only can improve your product, but also gain some respect from your team. Not only will they be inspired to avoid this kind of mistake again, they will also be inspired to think about process improvements and taking risks.

Until the genetic scientists manage to create a perfect person who never makes mistakes, we will have to learn to cope with them. Stop playing games and get to work instead. When it comes to process improvement, there's always plenty to do!

Discussion Questions:

1) Do you agree with the statements the author portraits in this case? Does a Blame Game really go on at organizations?

2) Why should a project manager take responsibility for his/her group action, if in fact, he or she was not the one executing the failed task?

3) Would group reward, instead of individual rewards, be in light with the management style advocated in this chapter? Should a project manager emphasize more a group rather than individual rewards?

Chapter 2
Working as a Team: Fostering Learning Organizations

Knowledge transferring will only be successful when you are able to fully and effectively engage all of your people, with a technological system and within cultural surroundings where they can all be comfortable practicing it.

The transfer of knowledge among a learning organization is a complex task, and yet, vital for successful teamwork. If taken seriously, however, and having the support of senior management it can be accomplished. Not that I have met any learning organization in its fullest sense, I haven't, and I don't think I ever will. But such a generative learning environment is to be cultivated, even though you may never be able to become a truly learning organization. Achieving such a level is like achieving the fullest sense of personal humility, or even Zen. Once you believe and affirm you have reached it, you would have just missed it.

Nonetheless, organizational learning is very important for team building, in particular in the twenty-first century, globalized, fast-paced and multicultural business settings. Business executives and team leaders must be aware that if organizations are not able to cope with the rapidly changing business environment, which also encompasses technology and human behavior within the organization, it will die. I strongly believe that organizational learning is becoming as important to corporate teams as vitamins and minerals are to the human body: depleted of it, the whole system gradually breaks down and becomes ill, and if not replenished, it eventually succumbs.

Senior executives, and ultimately the board of directors, are the ones in charge of ensuring the organizations' regular intake rate of learning (vitamins and minerals) that is fed into their teams and organizational groups. Executives, in particular those with knowledge and information expertise, such as CKOs and CIOs, should then be responsible for designing, installing and maintaining these systems, including information systems and technology (IS&T), with the support and expertise of CTOs. The major challenge here is how this executive team will ensure the adequate amount of learning necessary for organizational teams to flourish. Mainly because many executives do not even realize there is a challenge in building genuine and successful teams.

Examples of the lack of interactive team loops of what Bob Garratt[1] called policy (customer focused), strategic (director/senior staff focused) and operational (staff focused) learnings include:

--The fact that a large percentage of U.S. government workers will be retiring in the next few years and no knowledge-transfer strategy is in place yet (even though the U.S. government is aware of it, earnestly working towards it, as its first-ever CKO was finally hired in the spring of 2001[2]),

--Or that the tragedy at the World Trade Center in New York (on September 11, 2001) unveiled a reactive step-up in airports and airlines security policy and procedures that were long due for review,

--Or even the fate of successful business icons that suddenly disappeared, such as Digital Equipment Corporation (DEC) and Data General, not to mention the Compaq/Hewlett-Packard mega-merger.

According to Garratt, these team loops of learning (and transferring of learning, I might add) allow the critical review of all levels of the organizational teams. Such continuous learning enables teams to sense and respond to the changes in its external and internal environments to ensure the survival and development of the energy niches that support it. This is a very holistic approach, much like nurturing a living organism, as most of the learning and transferring of it inside the organization is personal, private, very often uncodified, hidden and, most of all, a defensive way of coping with the effects of a seemingly non-learning employer and employees.

Building Teams by Transferring Knowledge

Why is knowledge transferring so important for team building? you might ask. Back in 1498, Wang Yang-Ming[3] was already saying that "knowledge is the beginning of practice; doing is the completion of knowing." The former Chairman of SAS Airlines, Jan Carlson believes that "an individual without information cannot take responsibility; an individual who is given information cannot help but take responsibility." The same is true for team leaders, and their responsibility in bridging the knowledge gap inside their teams. A key strategy in this process is the effective transferring of knowledge.

To bridge this knowledge gap, team leaders must realize that the utmost knowledge base in any team does not reside in computer databases, but in the heads of the individuals inside the team. The majority of professionals inside knowledge-based teams worldwide have college degrees. Many of them hold post-graduate degrees and a large amount of know-how based on previous experiences and specializations. The challenge is, how do you get each one of these professionals to share what they know, not compulsorily, but freely and openly with everyone else in the team? In addition, how do you get them to accept responsibility for their actions? Where should your focus and line of actions be? In my experience, it has to cover a multitude of areas, including:

---

[1] *The Learning Organization: Developing Democracy at Work*, HarperCollins Business, 2000.
[2] *Knowledge Management Magazine*, June 2001
[3] Wang Yang-Ming, *The Philosophy of Wang Yang-Ming,* trans. Frederick Goodrich Henke, Intro. James H. Tufts, (n.p.: The Open Court Publishing Co., 1916), *passim.*

- Identifying and targeting individuals in the team
- Knowing the barriers in the team building effort
- Having a code of ethics
- Fostering culture change
- Promoting Innovation by thinking out of the box

Identifying and Targeting Individuals in the Team

For any successful knowledge transfer activity, it is important for you to identify the individuals from whom you need capital knowledge transferred. Unfortunately, I find that the more important the transfer of knowledge is, and the capturing for that matter, more difficult it is to identify and locate these professionals in the team, never mind get them sharing what they learn or know. Take, for instance, global consulting companies. To locate their professionals can be hard at times. Often, if you were to weigh the average amount of time professional consultants spend between offices across the country and the globe, at any point in time, you may find that 86 percent of them will be outside the office and many times outside of the country.

In a team where the office is not the place where business is conducted, knowledge transfer can be a very hard job to accomplish. The same is true for any other team, maybe not at such high levels as the professional consulting industry. For instance, if I am in my office for 40 hours a week, then my time in the office is less than 25 percent of my available time. If I consider the times I am working from home or a hotel room, then the percentage falls even further. Among the big four consulting firms, you may find that their consultants are in the office less than 14 percent of their available time.

Therefore, knowing where your team members are and how they will contribute to the transfer of knowledge is very important, and must be taken into consideration before you establish a team building and collaboration strategy.

Knowing the Barriers in the Team Building Effort

What are the barriers you are likely to face in attempting to build (or rebuild!) your team and implement a knowledge-transferring environment? These barriers are real, and they exist in every team. A typical one is the structural barriers of hierarchical teams, such as departments, groups and divisions, etc. Different operating companies in different countries, language, and cultural barriers are often present as well. There are many more barriers in building a team that will tend to be multicultural and geographically displaced, and you must take the time to identify them and have a strategy to overcome each one of them prior to any knowledge transferring initiative.

In order for any knowledge transfer initiative to be successful, you must not focus your efforts on a specific team, but on the whole organization, across all of those interdepartmental barriers. To do this you will have to focus on increasing the ability of team members in communicating their thoughts to others in the team, as it would be the collective result of a lot of individual actions that would be necessary to produce a result for the entire corporation. The question is how do you increase the power of these individuals to share their thoughts with others in the team?

There are many areas you should concentrate in attempting to become a learning organization (or team) and striving to transfer knowledge at the same time. One of the main areas of attack should include:

- Increasing the power of individuals to share their thoughts

- Overcoming the team's organization barriers

Increasing the Power of Individuals to Share Their Thoughts

Typically, most teams gather information on the front line, and then pass it to someone next to them up the line. The process then continues further up the line, with each individual team member adding some perspective to make it better. Finally it reaches some guru who gives the information the benefit of his infinite wisdom, typically an executive, an officer within the organization, and then the information starts coming back down the line or is stored into the knowledge base, the memory, of the company. Curious enough, in many cases the originator of the information will not recognize the information when it gets back to him, and worse, the information will not communicate what he had intended. If there was a system in place that could let the individual with the need for knowledge talk directly with the individual or group that has the latest and best knowledge, then this whole confusion could be eliminated.

For knowledge transfer to be effective among teams, it is essential for team members seeking the knowledge to be able to clearly communicate what they need so that the individual providing the information will be able to provide a rapid response to them. You can do this by radically changing the span of communication of the individual from his immediate work group to the entire team and beyond to anybody on any network that they need to go to for information. The greatest database in the team is housed in its members' minds, and there is where the power of the team actually resides. These individual knowledge bases are continually changing and adapting to the real world in front of them.

It is the role of the team leader, and KM professionals, to make sure to connect these individual knowledge bases together, bridging the knowledge gap, so that they can do whatever they do best in the shortest possible time, and without the risk of knowledge loss. I strongly believe that the greater the span of communication and collaboration that you give to team members, the greater the span of influence they will have. The greater the span of influence, the more powerful the individuals will be. If the span of communication is limited to a small horizon such as a work group on a local network, then the influence that the individuals can bring to bear will be minimal, the change will be minimal, and the benefits to the organization will also be minimal.

As you expand the ability of the individual members of the team, you expand the ability of the organization itself. As you change the span of influence of the team member, you change the power of the member and of the team as well. Buckman Laboratories, for example, was very successful in this strategy, by increasing the span of communication of their individual associates from their immediate teams to the global world of the company and to any place else they need to go for information. They gave their people access to the world, both inside and outside of the company.

It is this change in the span of communication of team members that provides the basis of the cultural change that organizations are experiencing worldwide. At Buckman, all those individuals that have something intelligent to say now have a forum in which to say it. Management can no longer hold them back. These people became obvious and respected in the organization based on what they can contribute to others, not how well they can please some boss. Furthermore, those that will not or cannot contribute also become obvious and can be intelligently eliminated from the team, and the organization.

Therefore, if you want your team to become a learning organization and increase its power in the marketplace, increase the span of communication, collaboration and knowledge transfer of the members of the team. Allow them to talk to whomever they need to for information. This is how you can improve the speed of response to the customer toward instantaneity.

Overcoming the Team's Organization Barriers

The team's organization barriers are a major factor responsible for the knowledge gap within teams. The collection of minds that exists within teams across corporate barriers, geographic barriers, cultural, and language barriers are great. It is necessarily to effectively transfer knowledge across time and space to meet the needs of the learning organization and ultimately, their customers.

Ideally, the knowledge transfer between the teams and its customers, as well as among themselves, should happen instantly. But this is not an easy task, and one near to impossible to fulfill, unless in very specific environments. But if you can reduce the transferring time, the feedback, from weeks and days, to few hours, or no more than a day or so, than you would have achieved a major milestone in knowledge transferring. The speed of response is a very important and measurable aspect of a successful knowledge transfer, in particular at the furthermost reaches of the corporation. This is because fast response time can drastically eliminate distance.

When you quickly provide a feedback to another member of your team or a costumer in a timely fashion, the distance between you and your office or your company and the customer becomes irrelevant. That's why many help-desk systems as well as customer-support services outsourced overseas, mainly in India, are so successful (many aren't, but for other reasons, such as ability to absorb local neologisms and cultural nuances!). The customer in United States doesn't really care if the solution to the problem is coming from the next town over or from overseas. All the customer cares is that the necessary knowledge required is transferred in a timely fashion.

Having a Code of Ethics

A code of ethics is the glue that holds a learning organization, any organization for that matter, together. It provides the basis for the respect and trust that are necessary in a knowledge-sharing environment. These fundamental beliefs are crucial for the communication and collaboration across the many barriers to knowledge transfer that exist in any team. A sound (and realistic!) code of ethics should be seen as an integral part of the effort to achieve and maintain knowledge sharing in a learning organization that your team should become.

Taking Buckman Laboratories again as an example, a clear code of ethics was key in their knowledge sharing implementation, because they were separated by many miles, and diversity of cultures and languages, which required a clear understanding of the basic principles by which they would operate. Some of these basic principles may include but should not be limited to:

- A forward-looking attitude about the future of the team should be constantly nurtured, so that generative learning, instead of adaptive, can take place, allowing team members inside the team to proactively control their destiny instead of letting events overtake them.

- All decisions should be made according to what is right for the good of the whole team rather than what is expedient in a given situation.

- Customers, and their total satisfaction, should be the only reason for the existence of any learning organization, and any team that embodies it. To serve them properly, the team must supply products and services that provide economic benefit over and above their cost.

- Each member's contributions and accomplishments should be recognized and rewarded.

- Learning teams are made up of individual members, each of whom has different capabilities and potentials, all of which are necessary to the success of the company.

- Members' individuality should be acknowledged by treating each other with dignity and respect, striving to maintain continuous and positive communications among everyone within the team.

- The highest ethics must be used to guide the team's business dealings to ensure that every member within the team is always proud to be a part of the team.

- The only way to provide high quality products and services to customers is to be driven by a total customer satisfaction motto --and not fear of being let go, or personal gains-- in everything the team does.

- The team's standards should always be upheld by the individuals and by the corporation as a whole, so that everyone may be respected as professional contributors and as a team.

- The responsibilities of corporate and individual citizenship should always be discharged in order to earn and maintain the respect of the teams.

- There should be a policy of providing work for all members, no matter what the prevailing business conditions may be.

FOOTNOTE

1. Knowledge Management Magazine, June 2001
2. The Learning Organization: Developing Democracy at Work, HarperCollins Business, 2000.
3. For more information about these events, check www.KnowledgeTechnologies.net

Chapter 3 Fostering a Culture of Change

Success often involves a strong internal champion, stumping for change.

How does a team leader create a team environment that maximizes excitement, creativity and a positive attitude, and minimizes the dampening effects of rigid resistance? How do you, as someone who has to adapt to change, stay flexible, keep your perspective, and capitalize on the creative opportunities that change can bring?

This chapter attempts to build the skills of the improviser (literally, "adapting to the unforeseen") in leaders and team members. This visceral experience of adapting to change situations generates support, a spirit of play, a sense of empathy for what it feels like to change, and most of all, an excitement toward taking risks and achieving new results.

Fostering Culture Change

Boards of directors and executive staff are responsible for the climate they create in the organization, the same is true for team leaders and their teams. Such climate has a major impact on the team's ability to share knowledge across time and space. Over the years I have seen this as the most difficult aspect of knowledge transfer to achieve among any team. By default, people have always taught themselves to collect knowledge over the years as a way to achieve power, or as a way of professional self-preservation, to say the least. What is taught in colleges and universities is that knowledge should be acquired and used, but we never learned how to share it. If teams are to be successful in this knowledge economy of the 21st century, we must reverse this tendency.

In this new economy, the most powerful individuals will not be those building their own "info-islands," but those that are willing to become a source of knowledge to their peers and their teams as a whole, by proactively sharing what they have. *Continuity* and *trust*, so necessary to accomplish proactive knowledge transferring within teams, must be promoted. Further, this same climate of continuity and trust should also be fostered with customers.

Aside from collaboration within the many groups of a learning organization, knowledge transferring also promotes the building of relationships of continuity and trust with customers. This fringe benefit of knowledge transferring is only possible if built by the team members. Thus, those with account responsibility, for example, are automatically involved with the customer by the nature of their position. Software engineers and product developers, as well as applications experts and industry specialists should be involved in this process as well, provided they are effectively engaged in the front line.

This is also true for everyone outside the team, who is a member of the corporate organization. Actually, the number of people in the team involved on relationships with customers can effectively determine the momentum of the whole organization in not only how efficiently it becomes a learning organization, but proficiently it exercises the transfer of knowledge.

Another important aspect to consider is with regard to the quality of the professionals in your team that you, as a team leader, can bring to this relationship with partners, supply chain and distribution channels, which will determine the level at which your entire organization can operate in this relationship. The higher the quality of the individuals engaged in this knowledge transfer, the higher the quality of the knowledge that can be brought to bear on any problem that your customers and co-workers bring to you. But don't underestimate other levels of the organization, as every professional, independent of their role can effectively contribute to this team building and knowledge transfer initiative. At Buckman laboratories, their goal was to have 80 percent of their organization effectively engaged on the front line.

Such level of knowledge sharing/transferring assumes different shapes according to the organization it is implemented. It may translate, as in Buckman's case, as how to get as many team members as possible creating and transferring as much knowledge as possible, in the best way possible, in order to have a positive impact on the customer. Some teams may focus on making sure that there is a high level of interaction between the organization's members and paying customers for a measurable frequency and duration. For others, it might be to ensure that the majority of their team members actively use their electronic forums, web portals, chats, instant messaging and email, or even to ensure that they get their accounting right, which may include profit recovery activities, so that their groups measure up to this new corporate goal.

My advice is, no matter what the nuances, idiosyncrasies and specifics of any given learning organization, the goal of knowledge transferring strategies is to bring about the full weight of the knowledge that exists in the hardware, software and team members, in a relevant and useful manner, to bear upon the requirements of the customer. I believe that any team, as learning organizations, especially those that realized they must adopt a generative learning attitude versus an adaptive one, are doing a lot of these things already. But if they can get all of their people exercising knowledge transfer at all times, a tremendous power can be unleashed. The goal here is not to go after definitions, numbers, procedures or any other quantifiable business goals. It should be about team member involvement, commitment, creativity, passion, and ultimately the freedom to do everything the team can, and to use all of the knowledge it has, to make sure that they have done their best to satisfy their customers--inside and outside the organization--in all areas.

Knowledge transferring will only be successful when you are able to fully and effectively engage all of your team members, with a technological system and within cultural surroundings where they can all be comfortable practicing it. Only then you will have sufficiently addressed the collaboration and knowledge transferring issues of your team.

Promoting Innovation by Thinking Out of the Box

By nature team leaders are, should be, professionals capable of influencing others. As discussed in chapter two and more deeply discussed in later chapters, the multi-disciplinary background team leaders must have, greatly enhances their span of influence over diverse teams inside the organization and out. Therefore, team leaders today must be instrumental in bridging knowledge gaps inside their teams, in order to achieve faster growth of the talented people in the company, to promote new ideas, innovation of thinking and ultimately to help the learning organization to think out of the box. Such professionals can influence others across time and space with the resultant increase in morale as well.

Team leaders are not the only ones responsible for fostering innovation among the team. Many other professionals within the organization also contribute, beginning with the Board, executive staff and technologists. The fact is, everyone in a learning organization should be able to promote innovation within the teams. The important it to realize that, to achieve these benefits everyone in the team must accept the fact that radical and rapid change will be part of the learning organization's life. Thus, consider these best practices facts:

- No matter who or where team members are in the world, everyone should be able to contribute to solutions of any problems in the organization, regardless of its nature or where it occurs. The challenge is to structure the team to recognize this fact. Another challenge is to structure this new learning team around the flow of knowledge, rather than geography.

- You must be sure to build teams that trust each other so that they can function effectively without an office, a department, a central core. This means to enable team members to be effective even while roaming, at a hotel room, at home, at the airport, at a satellite office. In other words, you must be able to move the team (and the office!) to where the people are, anywhere and anytime. Done? Now it is time to move the entire organization to wherever it is needed at any point in time-- without affecting the knowledge flow.

- In this new knowledge economy, where customers are much more aware of sales and services processes, speed in responding to them is vital if you want to remain competitive in the marketplace. Thus, here you have another challenge: to make sure the farthest groups and individuals within your team have the same speed of response as everyone else.

- Make sure everyone is engaged with customers or potential ones. Otherwise, what is the reason to have them around?

- Every individual's ability to acquire and use knowledge is very important to any team building process. Therefore, the quality of the professionals you hire is critical to the future of this new learning team. What are in the collection of minds of the team members determines how well the team will function. In this process, watch for reactions coming from the human resources group. You may find your organization in the need to hire teachers, coachers.

- If everybody is critically important to the organization's ability to close the gap between the know-how of the organization and the how-to serve the customer, then what needs to happen so that the minds of your associates can be expanded, so that they can be the best that they can be? Ask yourself how you can deliver learning anytime, anywhere. You may rely on programs such as

The Learning Space, developed by The Lotus Institute as an application under Lotus Notes and the Global Campus initiative of IBM. Or even this author's site, MGCGOnline, by MGCG, at www.mgcgonline.com. Organizations like these offer a variety of courses, and they can also customize one for you, at no extra charge!

To reap the benefits of knowledge transfer, you should invest in it like any other investment that will change the organization. It requires active entrepreneurial support from the Board and executive staff down to junior associates. Knowledge transfer, as well as knowledge management as a whole, resumes in culture change. And if you want to change the culture of a team, the leader of that team must lead it. If you want culture change in a team, then the head of that team has to lead it. This means the team leader needs to hold the flag, by adopting the changes, by using latest hardware and software for communications, by being open and accepting changes.

Remember, everybody in the team (and the organization as a whole!) will be watching. If the team leader does not walk the walk, then the rest of the team will not see it as important and will not adopt the changes either. Make sure that whatever statement of direction you have, that it is backed up with actions, otherwise, nothing will happen in the organization.

Therefore, keep in mind that knowledge transfer is more than collaboration with industry on specific products or technologies with commercial potential. It is a long-term process that establishes symbiotic ties between industrial and academic researchers. Transfer of knowledge can be further achieved through education, outreach, publications, workshops, and an array of other means.

Important vehicles for knowledge transfer are workshops and symposia that highlight research achievements to a targeted audience from industry, academia and government, and that allow group discussion on topics with broad impact and long-term importance. Through these meetings, center researchers disseminate information to a large audience and build research collaborations. They also introduce new technologies and provide hands-on training in new methodologies.

KM Strategies to Foster Knowledge Transfer in Teams

Learning must be turned into action in order to be effective. A learning organization (or team) is a breathing organism, and if it is not flourishing, it is dying. Thus, knowledge performance is achieved by valuing and using the knowledge of the organization on the job, turning learning into action. You might be in for a surprise here, but do the people of the organization know how to create value and make money for the company? If so, do they know what kind of knowledge they need to do this?

Just as any professional sports team, players have their strengths and their weaknesses. They perform better in one position rather than others. As part of becoming a learning team, you might have to deal with miscast positions, as well as not-so-fit ones. The way employees deal with knowledge, and the positions they hold, can mean the difference between your organization's success and failure. Thus, be prepared to conduct some knowledge performance targets to match your team members' strengths with the right role within the team.

Therefore, building a KM strategy is often the best starting point when attempting to implement a knowledge-transfer strategy within a team and the whole organization. The implementation will require you to know and understand what knowledge and systems the organization needs to enhance for its competitive advantage. There are six key components in KM you must address:

- KM Applications
- Intuitive Content Management
- KM Culture
- KM-based Governance

KM Applications

There are several KM and knowledge technologies you should consider in fostering knowledge transfer within learning teams and across KM communities. The United Kingdom's Knowledge Media Institute, at the Open University in Milton Keynes is a good place to start in searching for a variety of KM application strategies and tools. Nonetheless, I'd like to bring to your attention one of the latest methodologies in developing collaborative modeling, organizational memory, computer-supported argumentation and meeting facilitation, known as the Compendium methodology, which also includes a suite of tools.

Compendium has three key elements: a shared visual space where ideas can be generated and analyzed, a methodology that allows the exploration of different points of view, and a set of tools for quickly and easily sharing data both within and beyond the boundaries of the group. The process enables people to negotiate collective understanding "on the fly," capture the discussions, and share representations of their knowledge digitally across communities of practice -- an approach crucial in keeping collaborative efforts on track and on time.

The methodology is a result of over a decade of research and development, in particular in the UK, and offers innovative strategies for tackling several of the key challenges in managing knowledge and its applications, including:

- The improvement of communication between disparate teams tackling ill-structured problems
- Real-time capture and integration of hybrid material, including both predictable/formal and unexpected/informal, into a reusable group memory
- Transforming the resulting resource into the right representational formats for different stakeholders.

An Overview of Compendium

Compendium was first developed back in 1993 to aid cross-functional business process redesign (BPR) teams, and has been applied in several projects in both industry and academic settings[1]. As defined by Sierhuis and Selvin[2], Compendium was originated as an attempt to solve the problem of creating shared understanding between team members during meetings and brainstorm sessions in war rooms, typically working over weeks or months on the design of business processes,[3] while also keeping track of a plethora of ideas, issues, and conceptual interrelationships. Compendium allowed them to keep track of it all without sifting through piles of easel sheets, surfacing and tracking design rationale, and allowed them to stay on track and updated on a project's overall structure and goals.

Compendium is particularly effective in a face-to-face meeting, which is potentially the most pervasive knowledge-based activity in the workplace, but also one of the hardest to do well in the light of KM and knowledge transfer. Under the Compendium perspective, such meetings and brainstorm sessions can:

- Turn into untapped knowledge-intensive events, instead of unfocused, as they typically are, as they can be improved with facilitated application tools that help participants express and visualize views in a shared, common display
- Become more tightly woven into the fabric of work, as they are preceded and followed by much other communication and the generation of associated artifacts.

Intertwining the process and products of meetings into this broader web of activity should be a priority to any learning organization wanting to effectively improve the knowledge transferring process.

Researchers have found that a combination of facilitation with visual hypertext tools can improve potentially unproductive or explosive meetings between multiple stakeholders with competing priorities. This is possible by the capturing of diverse perspectives, which can also be structured and integrated in such a way that all participants collectively have ownership of these perspectives, as a record of their discussions. Such an approach enables a structured group memory that shows where the same concepts have been discussed in different contexts, why decisions were made, and allows one to harvest related concepts from multiple meetings in a form of conversational maps.

In addition, these conversational maps, designed to support the granular representation of concepts, as hypertext database objects, can be spatially organized, recombined and reused in multiple contexts, and can be integrated with pre- and post-meeting activities and documents. Development efforts are under way to convert material in conventional applications such as written documents, emails and spreadsheets into concept maps, so that their contents can be analyzed in new ways, and integrated with other maps.

---

[1] For more information, I suggest you visit www.kmi.open.ac.uk/sbs/csca/cscl99

[2] As in the white paper "A Framework for Object Oriented Performance Analysis," Florida State University, 2002.

[3] "Towards a Framework for Collaborative Modeling and Simulation," Workshop on Strategies for Collaborative Modeling and Simulation, CSCW'96:ACM Conference on Computer-Supported Cooperative Work ,Boston, MA, USA, 1996

Compendium[4] is an excellent tool in enabling groups to collectively elicit, organize and validate information required by a particular community for a particular purpose, by integrating it with pre and post-meeting processes and artifacts, through the generation of maps that can be transformed into other document formats, enabling asynchronous discussions around the contents of maps, and other forms of computation and analysis. I believe that the domain independence of Compendium's mapping technique for meetings, combined with its interoperability with domain-specific applications, provide a powerful technique for knowledge construction and negotiation.

Compendium is represented by a series of techniques revolving around a graphical hypermedia system for the development and application of question-oriented templates, which serve as semiformal ontologies to structure the subject matter of a particular project, as shown in figure 3.1.

See Figure 3.1 – Compendium question template representing the concerns of a particular stakeholder group

It also comprises a set of metadata codes that can be assigned to any concept in a database, as depicted in figure 3.2. The approach in itself enables the ability to move between formal and prescribed representations and informal, ad hoc communication, incorporating both in the same view if that is helpful to the participants. In addition, hypertext nodes and links can be added either in accordance with templates or in an opportunistic fashion.

See Figure 3.2 – Optional metadata codes added of a node assist subsequent harvesting and analysis of elements

Compendium's domain modeling simulation can be very useful in knowledge-transfer projects as it enables the development of a conceptual model first. Compendium is specifically good at allowing designers, knowledge engineers, and domain experts to collaborate on the development of a conceptual model of the system. Indeed, the benefit of a conceptual model in Compendium is the lack of syntactical and semantic complexity that comes with other conceptual modeling languages (such as semantic networks). In other words, answering questions in a natural language is easier than having to understand what the arrows and boxes mean in most other languages.

Another excellent product is Mindjet MindManager[5], which transforms brainstorming ideas, strategic thinking, and business information into blueprints for action, enabling teams and organizations to work faster, smarter, and with greater coordination. It extends core-mapping functionality with a host of simple tools--collaboration, distribution, and administration--making it easy for business professionals to quickly deliver bottom-line benefits enterprise-wide.

---

[4] For more information, check http://www.compendiuminstitute.org/

[5] For more information, http://www.mindjet.com/us/products/mindmanager_pro6/index.php?s=1

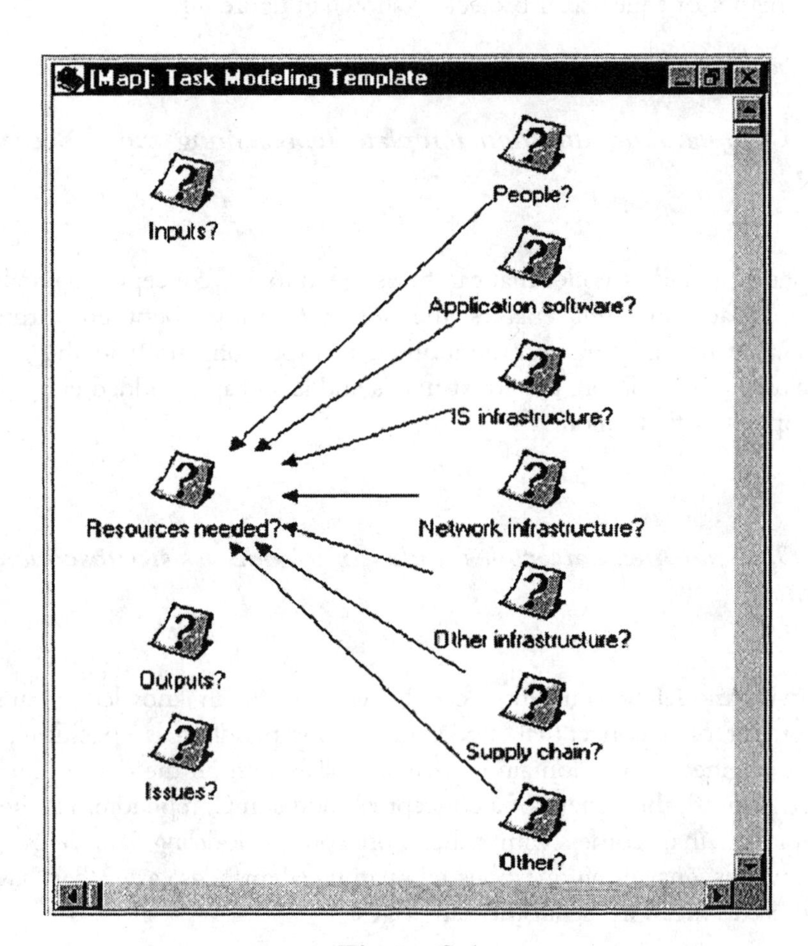
[Map]: Task Modeling Template
Inputs?
People?
Application software?
IS infrastructure?
Resources needed?
Network infrastructure?
Other infrastructure?
Outputs?
Supply chain?
Issues?
Other?

Figure 3.1

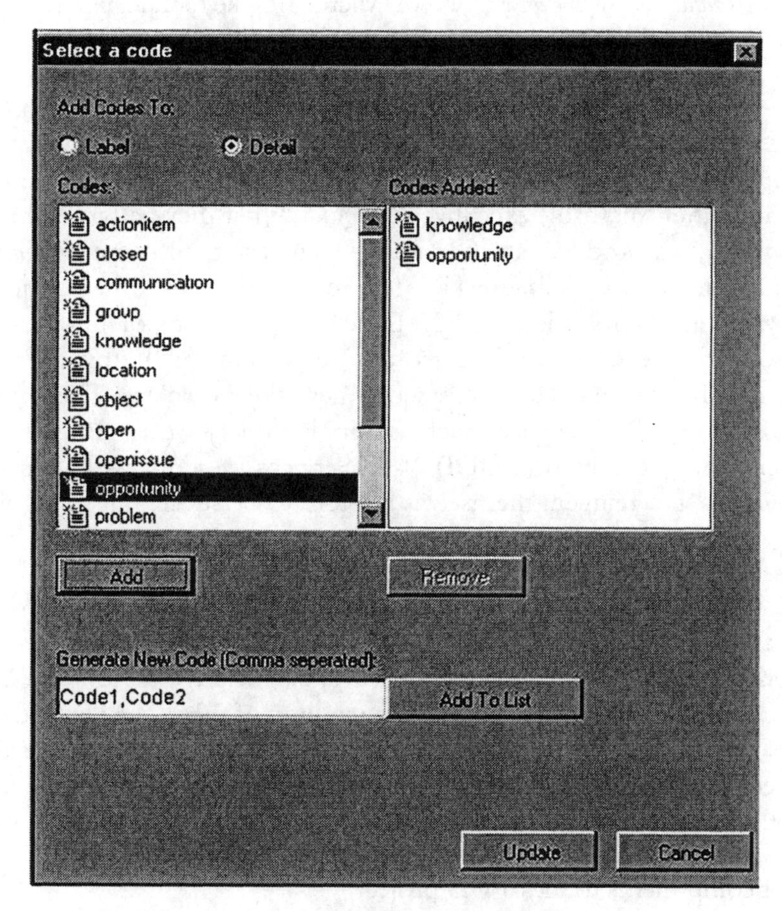

Select a code
Add Codes To:
Label
Detail
Codes:
actionitem
closed
communication
group
knowledge
location
object
open
openissue
opportunity
problem
Codes Added:
knowledge
opportunity
Add
Remove
Generate New Code (Comma seperated):
Code1,Code2
Add To List
Update
Cancel

Figure 3.2

Nurturing a KM Culture Inside Teams

When it comes to developing KM strategies to foster knowledge transfer in teams, Microsoft is a great example. The company puts great emphasis on its teams' capabilities and systematically acquires and develops the best possible knowledge workers for their given positions. Microsoft's Project Skill Planning "und" Development program, known as SPUD, focuses on human resource development, definitions, ratings, and linkages.

One of Microsoft's competitive advantages since its establishment in 1975 has been the quality of its people. Microsoft has always gone to amazing lengths to hire people with strong intellects and capabilities. As we read in the book *Microsoft Secrets: How the World's Most Powerful Software Company Creates Technology, Shapes Markets, and Manages People*[6], one of Microsoft's key strategies is, to "Find smart people who know the technology and the business."

Openness to change and the ability to foster cultural changes is important for any potential candidate to be part of the Microsoft's team. The company is always seeking high levels of competence as one of the main attributes, because of the fast-changing nature of the industry in which it competes. For instance, back in 1995, Gates and other Microsoft executives concluded that they had to embrace the Internet and incorporate it into virtually all products and services. As a result, software developers and marketers needed to be able to acquire new skills quickly. There was not any other option. Now, its entire organization recognizes that Web services and XML will be the bases of business transactions, office applications and information exchange. Microsoft is responding with the .Net platform, which is requiring the whole organization once again to acquire new skills quickly. The development of XML-based technologies to promote Web services such as Simple Object Access Protocol (SOAP), Universal Description, Discovery, and Integration (UDDI), Web Services Description Language (WSDL), and so on has required its personnel to reinvent themselves in order to be successful. Talk about radical cultural (and skills set!) change!

The SPUD initiative is being managed by the "Learning and Communication Resources" group within Microsoft IT, which also has responsibility for training and education for IT personnel. The goal is to use the competency model to transfer and build knowledge, not merely to test it. When Microsoft IT employees have a better idea of what competencies are required of them, they will be better consumers of educational offerings within and outside Microsoft. The project is also expected to lead to better matching of employees to jobs and work teams. Eventually the project may be extended throughout Microsoft and into other companies.

There were five major components to the SPUD project:

- Development of a structure of competency types and levels;
- Defining the competencies required for particular jobs;
- Rating the performance of individual employees in particular jobs based on the competencies;

---

[6] By Richard W. Selby, Touchstone, 1998

- Implementing the knowledge competencies in an online system;
- Linkage of the competency model to learning offerings.

Developing the Competency Structure

As soon as the SPUD project started Microsoft had already defined certain competencies they were looking for, but at that time, they were largely restricted to entry-level skills. The Northwest Center was also studying entry-level skills for software developers, such as requirements definition for a new system. These base-level competencies became known as foundation knowledge in the four type model used in the SPUD project, as shown in figure 3.3.

See Figure 3.3 – Microsoft's basic level of competence as defined in the types of competencies under its SPUD program

As depicted in figure 3.3 above, the foundation skills level there are local or unique competencies. These are advanced skills that apply to a particular job type. A systems analyst, for instance, might need a fault diagnosis competency for local area networks.

The next level of competencies is global and would be present in all employees within a particular function or organization. Every worker in the controller organization, for instance, would be competent in financial analysis; every IT employee would be competent in technology architectures and systems analysis.

The highest level in the competency structure is universal competencies, whereas it would apply to all employees within a company. Such competencies might be knowledge of the overall business a company is in, the products it sells, and the drivers of the industry. A course for all employees sought to provide general knowledge of the software industry and Microsoft's strategies.

Within each of the four foundation competencies there are two different types. Explicit competencies involved knowledge of and experience with specific tools or methods, such as Excel or SQL 7.0. Requirements definition competency, for example, is an implicit competence. Implicit competencies involve more abstract thinking and reasoning skills. At Microsoft, the implicit competencies are expected to remain quite stable over time, although with .Net, few ones are being added. Explicit competencies, of course, change frequently with rapid changes in fortunes of particular languages and tools. Within all four competency types, there are 137 implicit competencies and 200 explicit ones.

Within each type of competency there are also four defined skill levels. A team member might have, or a job might require, any of the levels below:

- Basic
- Working

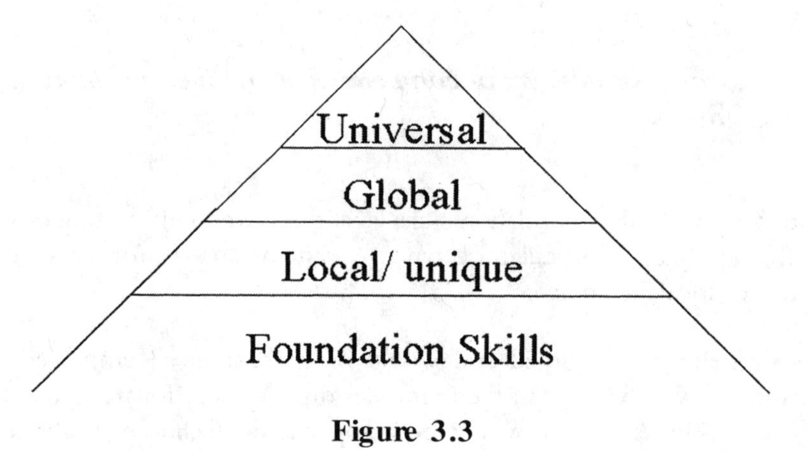

Figure 3.3

- Leadership
- Expert

Each skill level for each competency is described in three or four bullet points that make the level clear and measurable. The goal of the skill descriptions is to avoid ambiguity in rating jobs and employees.

The pilot for the SPUD project had gone well. Implementation was proceeding across geography and function, starting with the Operations function, then the Applications function, and all jobs in Europe. One issue to be determined was how the competency model might spread to product-oriented software developers within Microsoft. Many of the same competencies were obviously relevant in the product domain.

Developing Knowledge Sharing Proficiencies

For a learning team to foster knowledge sharing it must become proficient in collaboration. To do that the team must be able to shift from a culture where hoarding knowledge is power, to one where sharing knowledge is power. This is not an easy task, as individuals are the ones holding the knowledge and most often they feel very insecure about sharing knowledge, out of fear of becoming obsolete for the organization and losing value, which then generates the fear of being let go.

Therefore, the main challenge here for team builders is to get people to share what they know. Sharing is the basis of collaboration among people and any learning organization. Curiously, people across teams often do not know what it means to share and use knowledge. So, team leaders must educate and empower the team to understand the collaboration concept and get them going. It is imperative that a dedicated team is created, with special skill sets, to act as knowledge brokers inside the organization.

The following strategies of collaboration offer different benefits to a team building efforts. Beware these models require special manners and measures of team building support, and the more models an organization adopts, greater are the chances of becoming a successful learning organization

- **Meeting and Working the Network of Collaboration** - This collaboration strategy usually commences with a face-to-face meeting, a strategy or brainstorm meeting, a business or social gathering, or even a telephone call or e-mail exchange. Two people meet, identify some synergies, identify value in each other, and then resolve to keep in touch. Although collaboration at this stage doesn't yet exist, it has a lot of potential. If the strategy is successful, over time these two people will trade stories and backgrounds, compare acquaintances, unearth each other's skills, interests, and areas of expertise. Furthermore, they might build trust and rapport, even though they may not even, at that stage, have any interest in helping one another. But they remain open to the possibilities that may arise to possibly working together on a project, or to the possibility of sharing some valuable knowledge.

  Such process is far beyond the organization's control, as at this level, the process is still highly personal and often arises through serendipity (God set the times and the places!). This personal collaboration strategy requires very little technology beyond basic communications, is often unplanned, and little support beyond providing opportunities for exposure to others is necessary.

Executive education courses, seminars, symposia, trade associations, service organizations, charities, on-line discussion groups, book signings--indeed, any forum where interesting people congregate--provide rich environments for creating relationships.

- **User Groups and Task Forces: A Need for Collaboration** – Collaboration here is premeditated, as there was a need to focus on a very particular subject or object. Typically, this type of collaboration assumes the form of user groups, focus groups, task forces and so on, because a group or individual lacks all the skills or resources necessary to accomplish the desired outcome. For instance, President Reagan appointed a panel to investigate the explosion of the space shuttle Challenger. One panelist, Dr. Richard Feynman, used a cup of ice water and a strip of rubber to demonstrate that the explosion occurred because a rubber O-ring had failed at low temperature. But Feynman only got the idea to consider temperature because Donald Kutyna, an Air Force general on the investigative panel with him, remarked to Feynman that while working on his car, he had wondered about the effects of temperature on rubber.

  Just by asking questions you can promote collaboration within your team. Bringing together communities of practice is also a more elaborated way to promote collaboration. This strategy builds on the serendipitous nature of the first (i.e., "I know a guru who can help us with that issue!"). But for active collaboration to start, or for such teams to form, people have to be able to find each other, and the life of these collaborating teams may extend beyond the current need, but it is more likely that they will evolve or dissolve as needs change.

Every team should have a consistent technological infrastructure, compatible messaging system, integrated hardware and software platforms with software version control, and a resolve to stay current with developments in technology. A typical technology package to support active collaboration should include voicemail and e-mail (and instant message), access to networked exchanges as necessary and keep an eye on personal area networks (PANs). It should also have an on-line subject matter expert registry, conferencing capabilities, and groupware. More sophisticated systems will add workflow enablement, language translators, knowledge-based systems, and intelligent agents.

Generation of ideas should be fostered in every learning organization. Translating great ideas into new contexts can save the organization time and money, while raising the average level of outcome quality and implementation. Of course, you may decide to modify previous inventions as they change environments, but that is OK. Velcro, for instance, has continually tailored its original product to include new resins with unique properties for specialized applications, inexpensive disposable closures for diapers, and heavy use closures like those on a blood pressure cuff.

The major requirement when transferring knowledge is to have a robust corporate memory, with a KM gathering and collaboration system for users to contribute or review ideas, experiences, and work solutions, as well as to access the contributions of others, which can search broadly across disciplines. Web portals are particularly suited to supporting such contribution and retrieval systems and for enabling unexpected connections and discoveries.

Footnotes

1. Technology developed by Virtual Access Networks (www.thevan.com)

2. For more information, visit www.kmi.open.ac.uk/sbs/csca/cscl99

3. "Towards a Framework for Collaborative Modeling and Simulation," Workshop on Strategies for Collaborative Modeling and Simulation, CSCW'96: ACM Conference on Computer-Supported Cooperative Work , Boston-MA, USA, 1996

4. For more information on the company's products and technologies for data extraction, normalization and redirection, check their website at www.thevan.com

5. By Richard W. Selby, Touchstone, 1998

Chapter 4
Going Beyond Team Building: The Art of Enchanting

The foundation of a great team is a strong bond.

The knowledge economy of the 21st century brings a very elusive future. Business executives do their best to proactively prepare for what is to come. However, by the time they hear it approaching, they often discover that it is still quite some distance away; or worse, it already passed! The speed of business today brings about what Evan Schwartz called a digital Darwinism[1].

More than ever before, team leaders need to be smarter, faster, more innovative, and more adaptable. They must be able to lead their teams with unprecedented vision and execution to keep pace with evolving technology and customer needs. As Schwartz writes in his book,

> *"The world's biggest companies are gazing toward a future in which much if not most of their purchasing, invoicing, document exchange, and logistics will be transferred from stand-alone computer networks connected by people, paper, and phone calls to a seamless Web that spans the globe and connects more than a billion computing devices."*

To succeed, team leaders must be able to surf the waves of business at Internet speed, before professionals and teams begin to feel alienated by automation and outsourcing. To be able to succeed, and get the loyalty and buy-in from their team members, a *leader* must become an *enchanter*, a sort of *wizard of odds*, not to say of Oz! They must be able to understand and take advantage of *quasi-magic* events such as "sending a wireless fax from the beach; reading, if not producing, a customized multimedia newspaper on a portable electronic tablet; conducting due diligence on a proposed corporate acquisition from a plane 35,000 feet in the air and then beaming the report to the board of directors in advance of his/her arrival[2]."

Any team leader knows how necessary and important leadership is. Leadership is the main reason why some companies, teams, and business ventures succeed when others fail. The credit or blame of any

---

[1] *Digital Darwinism*, Broadway Books, New York, 1999

[2] Extracted from Burstein & Kline's book "Road Warriors: Dreams and Nightmares Along the Information Highway," Penguin Group, NY, 1996

endeavor most often goes to the CEO, the coach, or principal of any organization. Thus, the factor that empowers the work force and ultimately determines which organizations succeed or fail is the leadership of those organizations.

However, one must not confuse management with leadership. Management can be defined as a mental and physical effort to direct diverse activities, with the objective of achieving a desired result. In this process you may include the practices of planning, staffing, directing, and controlling. Leadership, however, is a natural and learned ability or skill, combined with the personal characteristics necessary to conduct interpersonal relations that influence people to take desired actions. In other words, people, you lead, things, you manage.

But, how does a team leader create a team environment that maximizes excitement, creativity and a positive attitude, and minimizes the dampening effects of rigid resistance? How do you, as someone who has to adapt to change, stay flexible, keep your perspective, and capitalize on the creative opportunities that change can bring?

The bottom line is that everyone wants to feel that they are on a winning team, that the company is moving ahead, and that they are an integral part of the group. How to foster such a team is the subject of this chapter.

Going the Extra Mile in Building a Strong Team

Building the winning team requires more than just hiring a bunch of talented people. In the process, you must:

- Assemble a group of people who will work well together
- Develop a shared vision and commitment
- Physically bring people together in formal group meetings for open discussion of broad-based issues
- Encourage positive, informal interactions between group members
- Instill a winning attitude throughout the organization, and
- Watch for, and quickly try to reverse, team-building problems such as jealousy, cynicism, and defensive behavior.

Enchanting the Team: Getting Members to Buy into the Team

In the 21st century, customers are much more educated and aware of products and goods than ever before. They can go to the Internet and compare prices and specifications, develop a competitive report among the vendors who supply the product they want, and even discuss the technology and features of these products. Furthermore, customers are rating their experience and posting it on the Internet, influencing future customers to buy your product, or not.

Therefore, team leaders today must do more than lead. There was a time when the hard line style of leaders, such as Lee Iacocca, was necessary and would pay off, as it did, for some time at Chrysler. But as the third wave of knowledge began hitting the shores of business, hard line traits had to be replaced with traits of persuasion, cohesiveness, non-bickering and self-aggrandizement. Instead of commanding, team leaders (and CEOs) today must be able to coach, counsel, manage conflict, inspire loyalty, and enchant subordinates with a desire to remain on the job, beginning with their own direct reports and staff. In the words of former President Harry Truman, "[the] definition of a leader in a free country is a man who can persuade people to do what they don't want to do, or do what they're too lazy to do, and like it." That takes enchantment!

Not convinced yet? According to Roget's Super Thesaurus, to lead is to direct, show the way, conduct, usher, head, spearhead, and escort. Now to enchant is to mesmerize, captivate, hypnotize, and sweep one off their feet. Which traits do you think make more successful leaders? Competence alone is no longer sufficient for a leader's success. They must be able to enchant their followers to accept his/her leadership by gaining, through ethical means, the followers' consent to be led. Thus, leadership becomes an activity, an influence process, in which the leaders gains the trust and commitment of his staff and every employee in the company, all without any recourse to formal position or authority to induce the organization to accomplish one or more tasks.

To be successful in the 21st century, team leaders must become enchanters. They must be able to get people excited; otherwise, they will lose them in a bit. People willingly sign up to serve under chief enchanters. Ask Steve Balmer of Microsoft, and Bill Gates' first generation of executive staff, and consequently the whole company. At Microsoft people work long hours, under pressure, and in a very challenging and competitive environment. Yet, their loyalty and commitment to the company is unprecedented.

Another well-known example is Jack Welch, CEO of GE. Addressing GE's corporate officers[3] back in 1987, he commented that "the world of the 1990s and beyond will not belong to 'managers' or those who can make the numbers dance. The world will belong to passionate, driven leaders – people who not only had enormous amount of energy but who can energize [enchant!] those whom they lead.[4]"

Building a winning team will require you to not only show people, and the team for that matter, in what direction your organization is heading, but also to get them to buy into the direction you are

[3] In Crotonville, NY, February 2, 1987
[4] The emphasis on enchant is mine.

taking them. Otherwise you can not expect people to support a group if they don't agree with where it is headed, or worse, do not even know where it is headed.

More specifically, you need to convey to every team member:

- Your vision for the future of the team and its mission, goals and objectives.
- Your strategy for getting there, achieving those goals.
- Why this is the best strategy.
- Every achievement that indicates this team is winning.

Beware that this should not be a one-time meeting to discuss strategic goals and share announcements. You will need to constantly remind people what the organization and the team stands for, and that it does indeed hold a bright future for all members of the team!

Building Teams by Nurturing Them

Part of building the winning team is having consistent, scheduled group meetings. These meetings, or even parties or celebrations, with as many people as possible from the entire organization, will help build a feeling of solidarity throughout the team, a feeling that they belong to the organization. Take advantage of these opportunities to share successful stories, convey new directives, coach, and promote collaboration. Make it an enjoyable time!

But while the time should be enjoyable, it is also important to have everyone participate in smaller group meetings where some work is done or some decisions are made. This makes people feel that they are not just part of some big group, but that they are an active, important part of a team. For key managers, or people in your work group, try to hold an interactive meeting once per week. It does not really matter how you do it, but make sure not to overlook face-to-face time. This should not be a meeting where you just make announcements, or summarize the work that has been done and needs to be done, but a meeting where everyone has an opportunity to give feedback on substantive issues. The well-known former CEO of General Electric (GE), Jack Welch, used to hold informal meetings over the phone almost every day. But he also made sure to have more structured meetings once a week or so. These meetings were very interactive, to the point where questions where asked and answers were expected. By the way, when asking questions, do not waste your time asking what you want to know; that is a given. Instead, ask questions you are "afraid to know" the answers to.

Promoting Collaboration

Perhaps the most difficult part of building a winning team is encouraging positive, informal interaction between team members when you are not present. For decades, teams have flourished in the familiar settings of an organization, in the field, across boundaries. But there has always been a kind of "cottage industry" in which small, cohesive groups are the units that do the work, sometimes working with similar groups in ad hoc collaborations.

As business challenges become more complex (due to globalization, shorter time to market, more competitive marketplaces and other reasons), however, it becomes clear that certain kinds of business problems cannot be addressed in isolated silos or pipe-like teams. This has long been the case for certain engineering projects and research workgroups, which often require teams of substantial size that may straddle multiple institutions. What is really new, however, is the sheer extent to which the need for team collaboration has come to pervade team structures, particularly for those problems that require back-and-forth movement between the field and the organization.

Multidisciplinary teams are needed to solve virtually all of the complex and multi-dimensional challenges in today's business environment. Increasingly, isolated teams do not have the breadth, resources, or regional outreach to interact with other teams and enable them to address the major challenges upon which really effective work depends. The cultural challenge to team collaboration, therefore, is to go beyond customary ways of thinking and organizing, beyond traditional organizational and inter-relational boundaries (within supply chains and distribution channels, for example), to establish whatever kind of cross-disciplinary and multi-institutional collaborations are needed to get the work done.

In building teams that are also willing to collaborate, try to:

- Have team members take part in the hiring process of new team members.
- Assign specific projects for two team members to work on together.
- Try to arrange for close proximity of offices, or team organizations.
- Create an incentive-pay plan based on common goals, such as profitability.
- Have a specific part of the salary review dependent upon "interaction with other teams."
- Take your team off-site for formal meetings and casual get-togethers to build a sense of bonding.

Watch Out for Team Builders and Destroyers

Ideally, your team will be packed with team builders, team players. You can identify them very easily as they display the following attributes:

- Highly communicative
- Listen actively
- Care equally about the problem and the process of reaching a solution
- Do not personalize criticism of their ideas
- Value the organization's success above their own

- Have a contagious spirit of enthusiasm, confidence and creativity.

Nonetheless, there are numerous problems to be aware of that can rip the team-building process apart, such as:

- **Jealousy** - Be on guard for jealousy whenever a new member is hired into the group. Go out of your way to tell other team members how much their work is appreciated.

- **Cynicism** - Some people are just negative by nature. Others might feel your company can't possibly prosper, or just don't like small companies, big companies, or whatever. Be sure you are emphasizing the company's positive achievements to the group as a whole. Do not hesitate to confront any openly cynical individual and demand their behavior change at once.

- **Lack of confidence** - Some people lack confidence in themselves and view attacks on their opinions as personal attacks, responding with statements like "Are you telling me my fifteen years of experience don't matter?" Stop any discussion like this immediately and, in a private one-on-one meeting, patiently point out the defensive behavior.

Table 4.1 lists behaviors that can promote or destroy teamwork, which can be identified by team members and leaders.

Table 4.1 – Positive and Negative behaviors of team members and leaders

Promote Teamwork	*Destroy Teamwork*
Listen, strive to understand	Preach and moralize
Paraphrase	Cross examine
Stay loose	Be noncommittal
Express feelings	Put on a "stone face"
Be optimistic	Be pessimistic, cynical, skeptical
Share the burden of proof	Require others to prove their points
Accept early uncertainties	Insist on early precision
Value learning from mistakes	Demand perfection, point out flaws, blame
Be attentive	Act bored, use negative body language
Give early support	Force others to overcome obstacles
Look to ideas, minimize rank	Pull rank, give orders, minimize ideas from below
Look for many options	Present the "one right way"
Develop the responsibility of the group	Deny the group's values
Take risks	Be defensive, stick to the tried and true
Share "floor time" equally	Filibuster if things don't go your way
Follow due process	Ignore process, jump to conclusions
Stay calm	Raise voice, threaten
Focus on the present and future	Focus on historic faults
Use data wisely	Present factoids/anecdotes as data
Start sentences with "I" or "We"	Start sentences with "You" or "They"

Selfless Leadership

A significant issue related to business in wonderland is the impact of the background belief system or tradition which the organization may identify with. Co-leadership roles tend to be structured according to such tradition, be it prior experience acquired as the protégé of a team leader, or the dictates of a parent body organization. Whatever the tradition, co-leadership roles do have a significant impact on the organization's success. A good book to read on this topic is David Heenan and Warren Bennis' "Co-Leaders, The Power of Great Partnerships"[5].

Advantages of Co-Leadership

As discussed earlier in this chapter, co-leadership is particularly useful if the team is a complex and large one, with several groups requiring careful monitoring or support. Also, co-leadership can provide mutual support, particularly when one of the leaders is lacking confidence or needs to work on their group skills.

In an organization experiencing difficulties, the presence of both leader and co-leader can act to diffuse feelings of anxiety and tension, as well as providing practical support. Another advantage is that co-leaders can learn from each other, both through working side-by-side in the organization and in feedback sessions. This can be useful if part of the relationship is aimed at transferring knowledge and leadership skills, as Coca-Cola's former CEO went on to prove.

However, co-leadership may have a negative influence on teams when it is uncoordinated. If team leaders have different opinions and approaches for direction of the organization, this can lead to confusion and unease, particularly if an argument blows up between leaders and their co-leaders. This can easily escalate into a situation where co-leaders feel that they have to take sides. It's important in this type of situation for co-leaders to be seen as supportive of each other. This usually entails some negotiation and discussion between leaders and co-leaders about how they wish to present themselves to the organization. Effective co-leadership requires:

- *Leaders that feel comfortable with each other* - It should be obvious that, for this relationship to be effective, co-leaders need to feel comfortable with each other and develop a relationship of mutual trust, which takes time. Otherwise, any distrust between leaders and co-leaders can give rise to a feeling of relief among the organization's members when leaders are not present, or give co-leaders with a sense of guilt if he/she disapproves of what went on in his/her absence.

- *Leaders that work together & respect each other's contributions* - Co-leaders need to meet regularly in order to structure group activities, give each other feedback and identify any problems which might arise. The partnership needs to be one of equality, as the employees of any organization can easily perceive an unequal relationship between leaders. In situations where there are two leaders yet one is obviously doing all the work, or where leaders compete with each other, detrimental effects will occur.

---

[5] Wiley, New York, 1999.

- *Leaders that share common aims and objectives regarding the group* - Leaders don't necessarily need to share the same beliefs and perspectives in all areas - different skills, approaches and perspectives can broaden the resources of the group. However, if leaders' different approaches result in attempts to pull the group in different directions, this can quickly lead to confusion and tension in the group.

In addition, the size of the team and the number of groups it has will also influence co-leadership dynamics. An arrangement with two co-leaders and one other member may sound rather strange, but from my own experience, I know this is not uncommon in the wonderland. Unless the leaders are able to re-negotiate their status as regards the other person present, this situation can quickly become frustrating for the other member.

The Reality Factor: Assessing Good Leadership

Successful changes in any organization will depend on leadership excellence. Leadership is a vital catalyst for individual, team and organization growth and success. Co-leadership partners have a unique opportunity and a enormous responsibility to shape the future of their organizations in a direction they want, rather than be slaves to it.

One of the major traits of successful leaders is that they create a climate of trust among their peers and people reporting to them. Trusting relationships are vital in the new economy, particularly because leaders cannot be sure about anything for more than a few months ahead. Thus when these leaders ask their team to move ahead, they are actually saying they believe this to be the right action to be taken, although they are not yet certain about how it will work out.

Consequently, those being lead will only be able to buy into their leader's direction if they trust their intent. The following is a list of key behaviors and attributes which successful leaders portray:

- **The staff's interests come first** – Before you can win the trust of your followers you must give them reason to. Thus you must give, give and give, before you can receive. When followers can truly see that their leaders are aware of their needs and care for them, they commit. At this point, instead of hired hand, leaders will have willing followers drawn by desire. If you are this kind of leader you will derive tremendous satisfaction from the success of your team (as opposed to your own success!). In addition, as you care for your team players and inspire them, they will tend to be more successful and have a stronger commitment to you, because of their feelings of support. There is nothing more powerful than a team player that volunteers his work and sees the financial remuneration as just a consequence. As a leader, if you are not an enchanter and do not lead by example, then you are using people to further your own end and you will quickly be exposed.

- **Doing the talk, walking the walk** – It takes time for a team to trust they leaders. Although team members can act in the spirit of trusting their leader, only their behaviors and actions over time can really attest to their character. Thus it is very important that leaders keep their commitments and hold their team accountable as well. There will be times, however, that leaders (or team players) will find themselves in situations were they feel that they have not kept their commitment. In this case, leaders should be up front as early as possible about the reasons.

- **Being aware of people's feelings** – As pointed out earlier, real motivation and commitment comes from the heart, not from the head. That's why volunteers are powerful players. To reach your employees hearts you must care for their feelings.

  Don't underestimate the power of reaching for your people's heart, for being interested in what they do outside of work; their families, their likes and dislikes, their fears, their personal goals. This is definitely a win-win situation. Just like the stock market, you must make consistent deposits into the hearts of everyone in the organization. This way, in times of green pastures and emotional commitment, you will have a fully dedicated professional (emotional commitment = profit). More importantly, in times of hardship, be it through your mistakes as a leader, economic downturns or business realignment, their level of trust will sustain disappointment, hardship and even a business failure.

  Back in the late 80s, when I was a CEO at TechnoLogic, a system integration (SI) company, we were all traversing hard times in the American economy, particularly with the savings and loans scandals. I eventually had to realign the business and close down the SI activity of the company, but my team remained committed through the end, more than I would have expected. A couple of these people, a Brazilian woman named Beatriz Salles (my right arm) and another Brazilian, Victor Murad, an SI professional, stood behind me all the way. They forfeited their salaries for several months, and at the end were even willing to lend their own money to the organization.

  Even today, as I write this chapter, and we traverse another financial downturn, I see my company facing financial constraints similar to those I experienced with TechnoLogic more than 10 years ago. Fortunately, through friendship, genuine concern for people is paying off again, as I have had a key senior staff member approach me and volunteer to have his salary cut to help the organization traverse these times. Not only that, but during business trips he has taken the initiative to stay with friends, to eliminate lodging expense, and even shop for cheaper gasoline when driving a rental car! No money, BMWs or any other type of corporate perk can pay for this level of commitment.

- **Handling pressure and crises calmly** – Enthusiasm is an emotion every team leader should portray. However, while fear and panic are emotions generally understood among the organization, its leaders should never convey them, even if they are feeling it. Instead of running around like chickens without heads, leaders and co-leaders should save energy for thinking the situation through.

  When leadership runs into major decisions which must be made quickly, there is no time for enchanting to work, no time for thinking the situation through and preparing the organization. It is very hard, if not impossible, to remain calm in situations like that. As I typically say in such situations, we should worry about crossing a bridge when we come to it, not before. Thus in crisis, co-leaders should focus on the action to relieve the situation and continue to move forward. One of the main challenges in bridging the knowledge gap in any organization is worrying about tomorrow, trying to anticipate the outcomes of innovation. Well, if one could anticipate the end result of an innovation, then it would not be innovation but only a reinvention.

- **Being honest and truthful** – Leaders must have high integrity, which should be based on clear knowledge of their own values. They should be genuine about discussions with their team, even and especially in hard times and uncomfortable situations.

  Derailed corporate leadership groups are often caused by betrayal of truth. The lack of honesty among senior staff, deceit and dissention, are the cardinal sins of leadership and management. When reality does not match expectation, leadership is faced with a number of disappointments and disillusions on business results.

- **Not taking personal credit for other people's work** – If leaders want to lose the trust team members and the organization have in them, they need just take credit for something they have not done. Credit must go where credit is due. Nonetheless, collaboration and teamwork is a necessity. Effective leaders will work as a team and be leveled with the team. They should utilize a hands-off approach, leading from within or behind, as much as from the front. Recognition should come from the success of the team and the growth of the individuals within. It.

  Acting as a CTO at Virtual Access Networks back in 2001, I was responsible for the research group and innovations in the area of virtual access technologies and wireless. However, as a group, we were pretty flat. We used to call ourselves musketeers and charge with the motto, "One for all and all for one." But since that group was hooked on sushi, we decided to call ourselves samurais. As a group, we all worked together, trying to build ourselves on each other's strength and weaknesses.

- **Always being fair** - To be effective enchanter team leaders must always be fair, not exhibiting personal favoritism, inconsistent behavior, unwarranted status or perks. Leaders must also make sure to stick with the code of ethics and best practices of the company.

  Watch for your own biased opinions. In wonderland is very easy for us to believe whatever we want to. Thus, look for feedback. In my case, once a month or so I take my group for sushi and we go around the table asking each other how can we better serve each other, both at the professional level, with the project on hand, as well as on the personal level, so we can continue to grow in our friendship. It has paid off, and we have been able to always under-promise and over-deliver in our projects, often two weeks ahead of schedule and more than expected.

  I am personally proud of that group of samurais, in particular because we have managed to accomplish so much despite the different nationalities and cultures of the group members. Vijay Gummadi is from India, Thavoring Heng is French, with Japanese descent, Rick Castello is American, and I am Brazilian. As individuals and professionals we are many, but in wonderland, under a chief enchanter, we are one.

Chapter 5
Moving the Cheese: Preparing Teams for Change

***Change before you have to.*[1]**

Team leaders must have a good head for building teams - global teams, that is! The current wave of globalization in this 21st-century knowledge economy has pushed companies past the point where team leaders with international responsibilities can simply carve the world up into territories, putting managers in charge who are primarily technologists with a second language and a flair for regional etiquette. Thus, team leaders who understand the global strategies of the organization can help in partnering with businesses at the regional level, in order to consummate those strategies.

Multinational organizations are employing a variety of strategies to ensure that they have the star leaders they need, and team leaders can help, as long as they possess technical astuteness, business understanding, cultural sensitivity, and the ability to communicate well. Of course, those features are hard to find, as cultural issues are not a clear-cut as one would believe. Different cultures tend to view some fundamental processes, such as coming up with a vision or strategy, through very different lenses.

For instance, in my experience consulting overseas, the kind of leadership behavior I had to adopt varied from one region to another. Although leadership tasks typically don't change, how you get the job done does. In Brazil, in particular Rio de Janeiro, goals and task lists must be fully supported by consensus over administrative/operating meetings. However, in Costa Rica, you can order it done and the executive team will typically trust and support you.

Needless to say, there is a huge difference between running a project in North America and in Central and South America. This can be easily revealed in approaches to project management. Latin American corporations look to a starting point and build to the logical conclusion, while Americans start with an end in mind and work backward. While this generalization may not always hold true, it is a great example of the variances in how people of different cultures exhibit the traits that are considered hallmarks of leadership. If North American team leaders are looking across a multinational workforce for individuals who have vision, for example, that quality may show itself differently in potential leaders who are not from the United States. Given the short supply of professionals with the right credentials, team leaders

---

[1] Jack Welch, former CEO of GE

can't afford to have their cultural blinders on when searching the globe for the next crop of team builders and leaders. Rather, they must broaden their own cultural understanding so that they can recognize leadership in many contexts. Otherwise, they may overlook those who lead in ways that are appropriate for their own cultures but not typical of U.S. style.

A Better Team Builder in the Leader Within

Finding the leader within you can dramatically enhance your ability to become a successful team builder. Although this premise is true in any role in life, it is very important for team leaders. This is true because you must have passion for what you do. You must be committed to a cause, have a vision, energy and courage. If you look back in history you will find that all the great leaders shared this same trait. Such leaders as Jack Welch from GE, Lee Iacocca from Chrysler, Ray Stata formerly from Analog Devices and now of Stata Ventures, Bill Gates of Microsoft, Michael Dell of Dell Computers, and many others are perfect examples. I actually suggest you to make your own list of successful leaders, as one of the best ways to become an inspirational leader is to study those who are. If you can, work for one and learn from him or her.

Early in my career I had two experiences with people I would classify as inspirational leaders. One used to be my favorite boss, while I was with Recoll Management Corp. First, she was always accessible. No matter how busy she was, she made time for me. To me, it meant that I mattered. Second, she never solved my problems. Instead, she gave me guidance in the form of principles that could be used over and over again for different situations. Some examples: "Don't speed up the river, it runs by itself;" "Always take the high road—in the long run, it is the winning strategy;" "Win the war, not the battle;" "Success is vision in action." Third, she encouraged me by praising my strengths. It was up to me to use them to succeed. Last, and maybe most important, she "lifted me up." She made me feel I could do anything. Isn't that what inspiration is all about?

If you want to find the leader within you, and as a team builder inspire others, here are some characteristics to emulate:

- Authenticity - Say what you mean and mean what you say. Meet commitments. Be predictable. Set the example of what you want people to be.

- Caring - The ability to empathize with others and understand their individual motivations is a hallmark of leadership. Great leaders find many ways to meet people's needs. They care enough to expect a lot from their people, and they believe in them. They engender tremendous loyalty as a result. When someone cares about you personally it creates a solid bond.

- Charisma - There are leaders with low-key personalities who inspire great devotion, and there are also many who have great charisma, drawing people to them like a magnet through the power of their personalities. Either way, great leaders manage to find a common ground with people and build rapport.

- Confidence - Fear of failure is not an attribute of inspiring leaders. They take failure in stride. The best leaders can readily describe their failures; only the mediocre have none to remember. Learn from these great leaders and try again. Have the confidence to make the big decisions and move on.

- Connectedness - Inspiring leaders connect with ideas by listening intently with open minds and learning from everyone. They connect with people by looking at them directly. They see people for who they are and what they know, and not what they are and whom they know.

- Courage – According to Aristotle, courage is the first of all virtues because it makes the others possible. There is an element of personal risk-taking in the deeds of great leaders. There is also a willingness to take a stand even if it is controversial or politically incorrect. With this goes the willingness to take responsibility and accountability for results.

- Determination - Some people commit to accomplish, others try to accomplish, but great leaders are determined to accomplish. They know no boundaries. No matter the number of distractions, they keep their eye on the target. They see obstacles only as things you need to get past to reach the target.

- Passion and Vision - People are drawn to those who have a vision and a passion for their cause. If you really want to become a team builder, being a visionary and strategist should make this easy. The mix of new technology and the transitional state of business as this knowledge economy unfolds before our eyes makes exciting opportunities easy picking. If you like what you do, passion surfaces with no difficulty. You should then create a vision for others to see. Finding the words, drawing the pictures that capture the imagination is a skill that can be learned and practiced.

Moving the Cheese: Preparing Teams for Change

The title of this section was inspired by Spencer Johnson M.D.'s[2] acclaimed book *Who Moved My Cheese.* The book tells a simple and amusing story of four characters that live in a *maze* and look for *cheese*, a metaphor for what you want to have in life, to nourish them and make them happy. The story reveals profound truths about change that give people and organizations a quick and easy way to succeed in changing times.

In the story, two mice named Sniff and Scurry, and two little people the size of mice, Hem and Haw, who look and act a lot like people, are the protagonists. In the context of the story, *cheese* can be a good job, a loving relationship, money, a possession, health, or spiritual peace of mind, while the *maze* can be depicted as where you look for what you want, such as the organization you work in, or the family or community you live in.

---

[2] http://www.whomovedmycheese.com

In the story, the characters are faced with unexpected change. Eventually, one of them deals with change successfully, and writes what he has learned from his experience on the maze walls. When you come to see *The Handwriting on the Wall* you can discover for yourself how to deal with change, so that you can enjoy more success and less stress (however you define it) in your work and in your life.

Unfortunately, innovation has always been a primary challenge of leadership. Today we live in an era of such rapid change and evolution leaders must work constantly to develop the capacity for continuous change and frequent adaptation, while ensuring that identity and values remain constant. They must recognize people's innate capacity to adapt and create - to innovate.

While there are many management, leadership and economic theories on what the future holds, we can all agree there will be a great deal of constant and revolving changes. Leaders must be prepared to successfully guide their groups and organizations through change to survive, innovate and prosper. This preparation should first begin with an understanding of organizational culture and the levels of culture. Analyzing a group's artifacts, values and beliefs, and basic assumptions will shed insight to the actions and reactions of a group.

Leaders, in particular the executive staff, should understand they are the most important players in the organizational change process. Using culture, creating or imbedding mechanisms, especially what users are interested in, sets the tone for the organization. Thus, to be most effective, leaders must consistently act in ways that reinforce their values and the desired end state.

Through a human perspective, leaders can look at how to best match people's needs and skills with organizational goals. Power and competition for scare resources give a view from the political frame of reference. Finally, a symbolic frame of reference sheds light on portions of a group's culture, including symbols, rituals, ceremonies, legends, heroes, and myths.

Change should not be seen as disruptive or threatening, as it provides new opportunity and resources for organizations to improve themselves through their own creative initiative, by generating innovation. It will take continued leadership effort and attention at all levels to complete the job, and leaders must be completely committed to creating an environment of trust, teamwork, and continuous improvement. It is only then that the organization will be an enterprise that allows each of its employees to achieve their full, God-given potential.

As discussed throughout this book, to thrive in the knowledge economy, organizations must continually renew their competitive strengths. Dorothy Leonard-Barton[3], a consultant specializing in innovation and a professor at the Harvard Business School, argues that "every *core capability* that leads to success is also *core rigidity*, and strengths can quickly become weaknesses." According to Leonard-Barton, organizations must consciously invest in activities such as collaboration, experimentation, prototyping and the acquisition of technological knowledge from outside the firm. She also adds that *if all employees conceive of their organization as a knowledge institution and care about nurturing it, they will continuously contribute to the capabilities that sustain it.*

---

[3] In *Wellsprings of Knowledge*, Harvard Business School Press, 2000.

Anticipating and Promoting Change

While everyone would agree that the 21st century holds many unknowns, team leaders, in order to effectively manage, must realize that the knowledge economy is characterized by vast and dynamic changes. New technologies, in particular the Internet and knowledge technologies, as well as new regulations, directives, and resource restrictions, will be catalysts of change.

Strategy in itself is a powerful tool in bringing clarity to any organization, as it can help integrate and focus energy, efforts and resources. I place emphasis on charting team leaders to lead change in organizations because these professionals can take advantage of knowledge strategies where three other critical leaders in the organization would be brought together, as members of the changing management process. By bringing these leaders together, who rarely have ever sat at a strategic table together except for staff meetings, organizations are able to derive an integrated, focused, strategic force to their efforts.

Another key challenge team leaders are well equipped to address is the need for systems that integrate knowledge, technology and people. Such a concern has been pointed out by Jim Bair, research director with the Gartner Group, who comments that we now have technologies at our fingertips, particularly the Web, that promise to enhance access to information and make it more pervasive and ubiquitous. Bair argues that organizations must now incorporate people into their team-building efforts. Bair also contends that firms should place more emphasis on capturing the knowledge and expertise of their employees, and then ensuring it is effectively shared. "It is the uncaptured, tacit expertise and experience of employees that will make a big difference," he adds.[4]

Notwithstanding, any organizational theory research will tell us that to change an organization, leaders must first understand how an organization operates. That also requires an understanding of the organization's culture, how it was developed and how it was analyzed. Further, leaders must be able to view their organization from several points of view and perspective to understand how it really functions. Team leaders can play a major role in this process by helping leaders to unfreeze, restructure and refreeze their organization's culture as necessary. Or, if you prefer, remove, reshape and reposition the cheese inside their organization as necessary, in order to promote innovation.

Effective team leaders are the professionals who most help moving the cheese because of their exposure to leadership skills (hopefully), knowledge management techniques, knowledge technologies and the generators of knowledge: people, the Sniffs and Scurrys, Hems and Haws of every organization. This is a time-consuming process, which requires a great deal of effort and consistency. Often senior management underestimates and misunderstands it, trying to address such cultural issues with Total Quality Management (TQM) implementations, which can be very expensive, lengthy and ineffective. The United States Air Force, for instance, overestimated their TQM implementation and, as a result, more than six years went by and they were still working to complete their cultural change. While changes may be implemented fairly quickly, it takes consistent leadership commitment at all levels to complete the institutionalization process.

---

[4] In Knowledge Enabled Enterprise Architecture white paper at http://strategy-partners.com

Organizational change can be seen as a double-edged management sword. Any major economic, social or professional event in an organization can disrupt the flow of business and other functions within the organization. When change occurs, it can promote unity and tighter integration throughout the organization, or unleash a backlash of unrest and turbulence. Changes in a large enough organization can affect an entire industry. For instance, when we look at the sharp decline in crude oil prices in late 1998, we see that such an event caused a significant reduction of business opportunities for oil service companies. Later, the burst of the dot-com bubble also brought hard changes to marketing companies and the whole concept of real estate on the Internet. The knowledge economy is an economy that capitalizes on change, and unless organizations get ready for it, the price to be paid can be very high, as this new economic condition calls for boldness, innovation and risk-taking.

Changing One Step at a Time

Changes in a team not only take time, but also many steps. In the process, any attempt to shorten the steps or develop short cuts will only produce a false illusion of speed, and the results are never satisfactory. Change is at the core of the gap between know-how and how-to in any team. I believe that often this gap exists because, although leaders know how to implement changes, they don't feel easy about how to implement them, and so they avoid dealing with changes altogether. Thus, team leaders must help executives and leaders to realize that change is not only necessary to bridge the gap, but also the only constant they can count on when turning knowledge into action.

Whether it is bridging the gap between the know-how about a new technology and how to incorporate such technology, about the know-how of achieving compliance with a new regulation and how to implement it, change is the bridge that makes it possible. Know-how must generate strategies, but only change strategies will provide the execution plans of how to create effective and lasting organizational change to meet these challenges, as depicted in figure 5.1.

Figure 5.1 – Change is the bridge, the constant connecting know-how and how-to in the transformation of knowledge into action

Changes can come in many forms and forces originated from both inside and outside the organization. Bridging a knowledge gap within an organization will always require the implementation of new organizational structures, realignment, and often consolidation of organizational roles and responsibilities, and even the revision and restatement of the company's mission. Thus, change is always at the core of bridging knowledge gaps, of turning knowledge into action. The problem is leaders and senior executives often have the tendency to postpone change, typically though actions such as "crossing the bridge when it comes," which often turns into not crossing the bridge at all, or worse, burning the bridge! That's why expensive consulting recommendations seldom lead to change, as executives, despite knowing what needs to be done –often even before hiring a consultant!—are not ready to embrace the changes that will come about as they begin crossing the bridge from "knowing how" into "how to execute."

Figure 5.1

As John Kotter[5] states, one of the major mistakes corporations commit is not establishing a great enough sense of urgency in changing. "Most successful change efforts begin when some individuals or some groups start to look hard at a company's competitive situation, market position, technological trends and financial performance," Kotter says. Surprisingly enough, according to Kotter, more than 50% of companies he saw failing in the changing process did so because they did not have enough sense of urgency. Executives either underestimated the hardships that come with changes, in particular taking people out of their comfort zone, or they overestimated the sense of urgency they had placed in the process. Lack of patience, immobilization in the face of downside possibilities, concerns about defensiveness from senior employees, lowering of morale, and outlooks of short-term business results are all reasons for not embracing change, not wanting to cross the bridge, or as Spencer would put it, not wanting to deal with the fact that something or someone has moved the cheese.

Team builders are leaders first and foremost, and leaders lead, or co-lead, in particular in times of change. To do so, they must be aware of the intricacies and inner workings of the groups they interact with, or lead. Although leading can be exciting and challenging, at times of major changes it can be very frustrating, as organizations are made up of people, and human behavior can be very difficult if not impossible to predict. Change always requires the creation of new systems; it requires innovation, which is a great thing. But innovation demands leadership. Therefore, before team leaders can readily help the implementation of change in a group or organization, they must first understand what makes an organization tick.

Dealing with Resistance to Change

One of the primary sources of resistance to change is the organization's culture. Team leaders and other professionals involved with organizational learning are typically well aware of it. But unless senior staff and leaders understand what organizational culture entails, very little can be accomplished in dealing with the resistance to change. By definition, it is commonly accepted that organizational culture is a pattern of common and shared basic assumptions that the organization learned as it solved its problems of external adaptation and internal integration, that has worked well enough to be considered valid and, therefore, to be taught to new members as the correct way to perceive, think, and feel in relation to those challenges. David Drennan simply states it as "how things get done around here."[6]

When dealing with the need to change, to know who or what caused the need for change is important. Not so important, however, if you look at it proactively. Of course, it is important to know who or what *moved your cheese*, so you can both run after it or them and compete to get it back. This is what I call a reactive approach to change, which does not necessarily lead to innovation, as chances are your cheese was moved as a result of innovation, only not generated by you or your organization. Thus, you must move your cheese before someone does it for you, or as Jack Welch once said, "change before you have to."[7]

Successful change must lead to innovation. Otherwise, your organization is only playing catch-up. Often, failed attempts to change are a result of lack of vision. In such cases, you do find plenty of plans and

---

[5] In "Leading Change: Why Transformation Efforts Fail," *Harvard Business Review on Change*, 1998, Boston
[6] *Transforming Company Culture*, McGraw-Hill, New York, 1992.
[7] *Excellence in Management & Leadership Series*, Jack Welch, MICA Group, Canada, 2001

programs, but not vision. Success is a result of a vision in action. If your organization is pursuing change based on a vision, but is not experiencing success, verify your action plans, as very likely there is not much action in place, a result typically caused by resistance or fear. By the same token, if you believe you have a good action plan, have the support of the organization, and still you are not successful in implementing changes, and consequently innovation, you must check your vision, or lack thereof.

Always remember, innovative success is the result of vision in action. Some immediate actions that can be taken when managing change include:

- Create a new vision
- Define a mission statement, core values, basic principles, and an operating style
- Create a quality council of senior leaders to oversee the change process

Removing, Reshaping and Repositioning the Cheese

Organizations deal with change differently, depending on the stage they find themselves in. For that reason, the phenomenon in which knowledge managers whose organizational change projects start with great promise but fail to live up to that promise, and eventually do not make the grade as successful reengineering or even plain change, is unfortunately more common than one would expect.

Creative individuals stand out from the rest of us, and often have odd reporting relationships, but somehow they instinctively insert themselves into organizations wherever they are needed, and the changes and innovations they bring are often more like leaps than the small steps most of us experience. They think of the world in large terms, and their creativity comes from the novel connections they make between their work and their experience or observations. They are usually curious and need a field in which to exercise that curiosity. Leaders can work to bring the special and creative gifts of these people to bear on the efforts of a group.

Team leaders and knowledge managers are catalysts in this process, as knowledge strategies enable organizations to enhance their business competencies, whether focused on efficient operations, product innovation or customer intimacy, thus becoming an important component of removing and reshaping the cheese. By strategically managing and capitalizing on knowledge, organizations can generate tremendous value for shareholders and customers.

In order for team leaders to become effective instruments for change in organizations, they must realize that any organization in a growth stage has their leaders focused on the development of group values and assumptions. Thus, what leaders pay attention to, control, and reward, as well as how they allocate resources, select, promote, and eliminate people, is very important during this stage. This is a phase in the organization where there is a lot of personnel recasting, mission focusing and the establishment of business processes. Team leaders are even more important in the change process when the organization matures, as leaders begin to lose their ability to manipulate the organization, thus making it more difficult to enforce changes. This is a very sensitive stage for any organization experiencing change, as earlier strength can turn into liabilities, and often what leaders had believed to be an organization's weakness can very well become what was required of it as strength in a different context.

In addition, team leaders must possess two or three of the following characteristics, and help their executive peers, in particular the CEO, also to develop as many as these traits as possible:

- Ambitious – Do people in your organization perceive you as someone that has managed your career well over the years? Do they have confidence that if they stick with you they too can benefit from your successes?

- Excellent motivator and team builder – Are you a team leader? Do people easily follow your dreams, your directions, despite the clarity of your vision at times? In other words, do people have faith in you? You should always be able to develop visions of the future that are relatively easy to communicate and appeal to customers, employees, and stockholders. At times, however, one must believe what cannot yet be seen.

- Loyal and proactive management habits – Are you willing to make sacrifices for the organization and its members? Would you be willing to temporarily sacrifice your salary so that you could make ends meet in the organization? This is a trade a CEO must possess if she/he is to earn the respect and loyalty of their employees, especially in tough times.

- Outgoing, well-liked (enchanting) – Are you a true enchanter, a person that people like to hang out with, to listen to? Are you (or your CEO) seen as charming?

- Outstanding reputation – Do people in the organization perceive you as someone with a high level of competence and potential for success?

- Survived organizational restructuring or change of management – Do you have a history of surviving corporate shakeouts, which may indicate an inherit value to the organization and an above average emotional intelligence (EQ)?

- Technically savvy – Do you or have a reputation for being technically brilliant, insightful and visionary?

Having two or more of the traits listed above positions leaders for success in promoting change in their organization. However, as Edgar H. Schein[8] comments, leaders should be able to understand how culture is created, embedded, developed and ultimately manipulated, managed and changed. Often, many problems that were once viewed simply as communication failures or lack of teamwork are in essence a breakdown of intercultural communications. For instance, many companies today are trying to improve their designing and manufacturing process, as well as the delivery of new products to customers.

[8] In *Organizational Culture and Leadership*, Jossey-Bass Business & Management Series, 1997.

Removing the Cheese

Removing the cheese from the organization is the first step in seeking out changes and promoting innovation. The process of removing the cheese should be backed up with information or data showing negative trends or tendencies, proving that the current *cheese* is no longer healthy for the organization or its individuals. For instance, the organization is failing to meet some of its goals, or its systems are not working as efficiently as required.

Team leaders must make sure that this negative information is fully recognized and explicitly linked to important organizational goals, so as not to produce a feeling of guilt or anxiety within the organization. By using community of practice approach, peer-group discussions and other KM tools, leaders then must provide a new vision to serve as a psychological bridge from the current situation to the new one. Here again, bridging the knowledge gap created by changes in the environment or business landscape is very important. At this stage team leaders must act very cautiously though, with much regards for the well - being of the organization's members, much like dealing with a close relative that has just lost someone or something very close and dear to their hearts.

A leader connects creative people to the entire organization. A leader does not demand unreasonable personal or corporate loyalty, understanding that creative persons are loyal to an idea that may often appear to others as not so feasible. Their work rises from discovering and connecting. People remember the story of Archimedes' discovering the principle of displacement while taking a bath, because creative people have insights in all kinds of contexts. Art Fry realized the potential of Post-it notes while singing in his church choir. Hewlett-Packard began in a garage. Leaders understand the potential of connections like these and make it possible for creative persons to discover them.

The word *removing* can be a negative word in itself, pointing to notions of loss, emptiness, void and despair. Thus it is here, at this first stage, that most organizations give up on changing. At this point, all the organization knows is that the current state of affairs is not healthy, no good, and needs to change. But it is part of human nature to resist changes. Therefore, reshaping the cheese is a very important stage, one that will determine the success or failure of change in the organization, in which the pure essence of innovation depends on. Quality programs must be developed during the reshaping stage to review:

- The establishment or refocus of mission statements and objectives
- The creation of a new strategic plan
- The development of quality councils, to assess and re-evaluate the quality of staff in light of new mission and goals, thus preventing the miscast of staff, personnel and team training
- The development of process action teams, and measurement indicators or metrics
- The development of individual and team quality awards programs to be implemented during the repositioning of the cheese.

Also, during the removing of the cheese, make sure to include training as one of the basic components of quality programs. Training courses and workshops, ranging from awareness, team member and team leader programs, as well as customer satisfaction, teamwork skills, and continuous process improvement programs, should be included.

The organization's and employees' visions, missions, credos and core values serve as cultural embedding mechanisms. Thus, it is important that throughout the change project leaders continuously refer to, and reinforce, management actions by providing directions to guide action and change. A good idea is to develop frames and small posters to be affixed on the walls of the organization, as a constant reminder that they are all engaged in the changing process. It is when these espoused concepts and values are continually reinforced and discussed that the organization and its employees begin to move deeper into the new organization's culture, and impact basic values and shared assumptions of the group. This takes conscious commitment over time.

Reshaping the Cheese

With the organization's current (or obsolete!) knowledge system *removed*, leaders now must think about restructuring the organization's basic assumptions, the employees' basic belief system, and their basic knowledge base. Leaders now must reshape the organization's cheese!

At this stage, a clear vision for what the organization wants to achieve is very important. Without one, the changing effort can easily dissolve into a very confusing project, with many incompatible initiatives, which can dangerously take the organization in a completely different and wrong direction. Furthermore, the onset of a blurry vision will produce lack of cooperation from the individuals in the organization, who will not be willing to make any sacrifices, especially if they are unhappy with the status quo. At this stage, everyone must believe that useful and fruitful change is possible. Thus, credible communication consistently delivered is a must if leaders want to capture the hearts and minds of the organization as a whole. More than ever, at this stage, success will be the result of vision in action.

Team leaders can be very effective here by using gentle and consistently applied pressure on the organization about the vision, the actions to take the organization there, and the rewards that awaits once they get there. Some strategies may include:

- Lively articles about the new vision, delivered through the organization's newsletter. If you don't have one, create one!

- Replace the boring and ritualistic weekly staff meetings with exciting discussions on the changes being undertaken.

- Make change the core objective of the organization. For instance, instead of discussing sales pipelines, discuss what needs to change this week so that the organization can be more profitable. Instead of discussing performance planning and reviews, discuss how can individuals in the organization improve themselves on a daily basis, in all fronts.

- Most importantly, talk about how everyone in the organization, beginning with the CEO and the executive staff, can walk the talk. How can everyone consciously attempt to become a living symbol of the new organization's culture?

Keep in mind that communication comes in both words and deeds, and the latter are often the most powerful and effective form. Be careful with leadership behavior, as well as the posture adopted by the employees during this process of reshaping the cheese, refocusing the vision. Nothing undermines change more than behavior by senior staff that is inconsistent with their words.

Repositioning the Cheese

Finally, this new behavior and desired set of assumptions and beliefs must be continually reinforced until there is no more anxiety throughout the organization and in the system. At this point, the organization should be stabilized. Thus, in successfully repositioning the cheese, make sure to continuously involve large numbers of supporters as you progress.

Make sure to encourage employees, emboldening them to try the new approaches and develop new ideas in line with the new vision. The more employees you get involved, the better will be the outcome. However, do not rely on communication alone. Repositioning also requires the removal of obstacles. Often individuals in the organization see the new vision and want to be part of it. But very often, they get immobilized by a wall that appears in front of them, rendering their effort ineffective. Most of the time these walls are imaginary, present only in their heads. Thus the challenge is to be able to convince them that there is nothing, or no personal risks, to stop or prevent them from changing. Such walls can seem to be very real, as the human self-preservation instinct tries to avoid actions that are perceived to be detrimental to employment, image or career.

Another important aspect in repositioning the cheese is timing. Change takes time, so it is important the leaders keep the organization motivated throughout the process. Most employees will not stick around waiting for the benefits of change for too long. Thus, make sure to plan for at least some small results within 12 to 24 months. Without these short-term results, employees might begin to give up on the vision, and even display resistance against the changes.

Team leaders again bring an advantage to the change process, as leaders are pressured to produce short-term results. Since team leaders typically are not so involved with the management of employees and their everyday responsibilities, they fit very well in the role of *bad cop*. Direct managers do not like the fact they may be forced to produce short-term results for the changes taking place. At this stage, pressure can be very useful in achieving this goal, particularly because once managers and employees realize that major changes will be slower to materialize, the urgency level tends to drop. By not being directly in the line of fire, team leaders can help to keep the urgency level up, while promoting business intelligence activity that may enable the clarification or revision of the vision.

Finally, a successful repositioning of the cheese or a successful change in the organization is measured by how well the changes become embedded in the organization's new culture, seeped into the way its employees conduct their everyday business. As discussed earlier, an organization's culture can be summarized as the way things are done. By the same token, a successful change will be institutionalized throughout the organization, and become part of its culture.

To ensure changes are institutionalized in the organization's culture, knowledge about the change and the new way of doing things has to be turned into action. One way of verifying that is by consciously attempting to show employees all the positive results the new approach, behavior, and attitude have brought to the organization and its performance. It is very important that leaders make an effort to communicate such accomplishments, as employees may not realize this or may establish very inaccurate views of the results.

Closing the Circle of Innovation: Forget the Cheese!

In the knowledge economy, innovation is not only a necessity, it is king. Unless learning organizations gain access to new ideas that in turn can help the generation of innovation, timely dialogue cannot be established, promising ideas cannot be disseminated. But conducting business at the speed of thought gets more complicated than this, as different industries operate at different levels of change, and thus need to use different approaches to succeed.

The goal of every innovator should be two-fold. First, to forget about the cheese they have or use to have. Such cheese, be it a technology, skill set, customer base, current product or service, has been moved by market forces, competition, obsolescence or economic shifts. Thus, the challenge now is to forget the cheese and focus on creating a new one, which will require more than simply chasing the cheese or responding to its demand. Think about some of the many times cheeses were moved in the past few decades:

- Chrysler moved the automobile industry's cheese in 1993 with the introduction of the minivan. At that time, a van mounted on a car chassis with folding seats and cup-holders moved the cheese of every automaker and car buyer.

- Sony moved its customers, and the industry's, cheese when it told them to strap its tape players around their head, giving birth to the Walkman.

- Napster moved the cheese of record label companies when it forced them to adapt to a new way of distributing and selling music tracks over the Internet.

- Audible is moving the cheese of hardcopy book sellers and readers by making it available over the internet on MP3 format, allowing people to enjoy a book even if they are driving, flying, jogging, in bed with the lights off or in a group.

In this new economy, successful companies are not those capable of surviving the move of their cheese, but those capable of letting their cheese go so that they can search for more enjoyable and gratifying cheese. Innovation is the main ingredient to spark new sources of revenue based on changing and disruptive technologies, demographics, and consumer habits. Just like a new kind of cheese can destroy the demand for old ones, new business models can also destroy old ones.

Therefore, moving the cheese to promote innovation is a threat to every traditional, uninspired business. Never before have strategy life cycles been shorter and market leadership counted for less. If you or your company is not pursuing innovation, rest assured that it will be a matter of time until you become overwhelmed by it. Strategy innovation is the only way to deal effectively with continuous -- and disruptive -- change.

Chapter 6
Mastering Team Building and Management

The commonly held belief that those who haven't failed haven't attempted anything difficult holds as true for teams as it does for individuals.

Very often quoted, and also misunderstood, Doctor Bruce Tuckman's classic description of the five stages of team building is at the core of many organizational development programs, mainly because the model is easy to understand and remember. As a respected educational psychologist, Tuckman first described the (then) four stages of team building in 1965, soon after leaving Princeton. As already mentioned in chapter 1, looking at the behavior of small groups in a variety of environments, he recognized the distinct phases team members go through, and suggested they need to experience all four stages before they achieve maximum effectiveness. He refined and developed the model in 1977 with the addition of a fifth stage, adjourning.

The Forming, Storming, Norming, Performing (and Adjourning) theory is very helpful in explaining team development and behavior. You will find striking similarities between his model and others, such as the Tannenbaum and Schmidt Continuum, and especially Hersey and Blanchard's Situational Leadership® Model, which was developed at about the same time.

Tuckman's model does an excellent job in demonstrating that as the team develops maturity and ability, relationships are established, and the leader will change leadership style. Team leaders should use a directing style of leadership at early stages of team development, but should move on to coaching and then participating. At this point, the team members should be a lot more independent than before, which allows leaders to begin delegating tasks and eventually be able to almost detach themselves from the team. It is common, at this point, for teams to produce a successor leader, who will rise from among the group, at which point the previous leader can move on to develop a new team.

This progression of team behavior and leadership style can be seen clearly in the Tannenbaum and Schmidt Continuum - the authority and freedom extended by the leader to the team increases while the control of the leader reduces. In Tuckman's Forming, Storming, Norming, Performing model, Hersey's and Blanchard's Situational Leadership® model, and in Tannenbaum and Schmidt's Continuum, we see the same effect, represented in three ways.

When building teams, there are several favorable conditions for developing high performance which be noticed, including:

- Restrict teams as much as possible to no more than ten members
- Team membership should be voluntary
- Service on the team should be continuous
- Assign leaders full-time to the team
- Nurture an organizational culture of cooperation and trust
- Members should report only to the team leader (dual or multiple leaders will confuse the team and increase the risk for dissension)
- Make sure to represent all relevant functional areas on the team
- Team projects should always have a compelling objective
- Members should always be in speaking distance of each other (conditions for building successful virtual teams will be discussed in chapter 9).

Understanding the Team Development Phases

Tuckman described the five distinct stages in which a team develops as it comes together and starts to operate. This process can be subconscious, although an understanding of the stages can help the team reach effectiveness more quickly and less painfully. Already mentioned in chapter 1, these stages are:

1. Forming
2. Storming
3. Norming
4. Performing
5. Adjourning

Figure 6.1 depicts the five phases of team development as described by Tuckman. You might want to examine the figure as you read about the features of each phase discussed below.

Figure 6.1 – Tuckman's Five Team Development Phases

The Forming Phase

In the forming phase, there is high dependence on leaders for guidance and direction. There is little agreement on team aims and objectives, other than those received from the leader. At this stage, individual roles and responsibilities are unclear, so leaders must be prepared to answer lots of questions about the team's purpose, objectives and external relationships.

Also in this stage, there will not be much focus on processes, which will often be ignored; beware that team members will tend to test the tolerance of the system and the leader. It is therefore important for leaders in this phase to *direct* the team.

The Storming Phase

During this phase, the impression one has is that chaos reins. Decisions will not come easily within the team. Team members will compete for position as they attempt to establish themselves in relation to other team members and the leader, who might receive challenges from team members. Although at this phase there will be more clarity of purpose, there will also still be plenty of uncertainties throughout the team.

Cliques and factions tend to form, and power struggles can be very common. It is very important that the team be focused on its goals to avoid becoming distracted by relationships and emotional issues. Compromises may be required to enable progress. In this phase, leaders should shift style from directing to coaching.

The Norming Phase

In this phase, agreement and consensus is largely formed among teams. Members tend to respond well to facilitation by the leader and, therefore, roles and responsibilities can be clarified and accepted. Also in this phase, it becomes possible for big decisions to be made by team agreement. Smaller decisions may be delegated to individuals or small teams within the group.

The norming phase also is characterized by commitment and unity of the team, which tends to be very strong. The team may engage in fun and social activities. The team discusses and develops its processes and working style. There is general respect for the leader and more leadership is shared by the team. Again, at this stage, leaders should shift from coaching to facilitation.

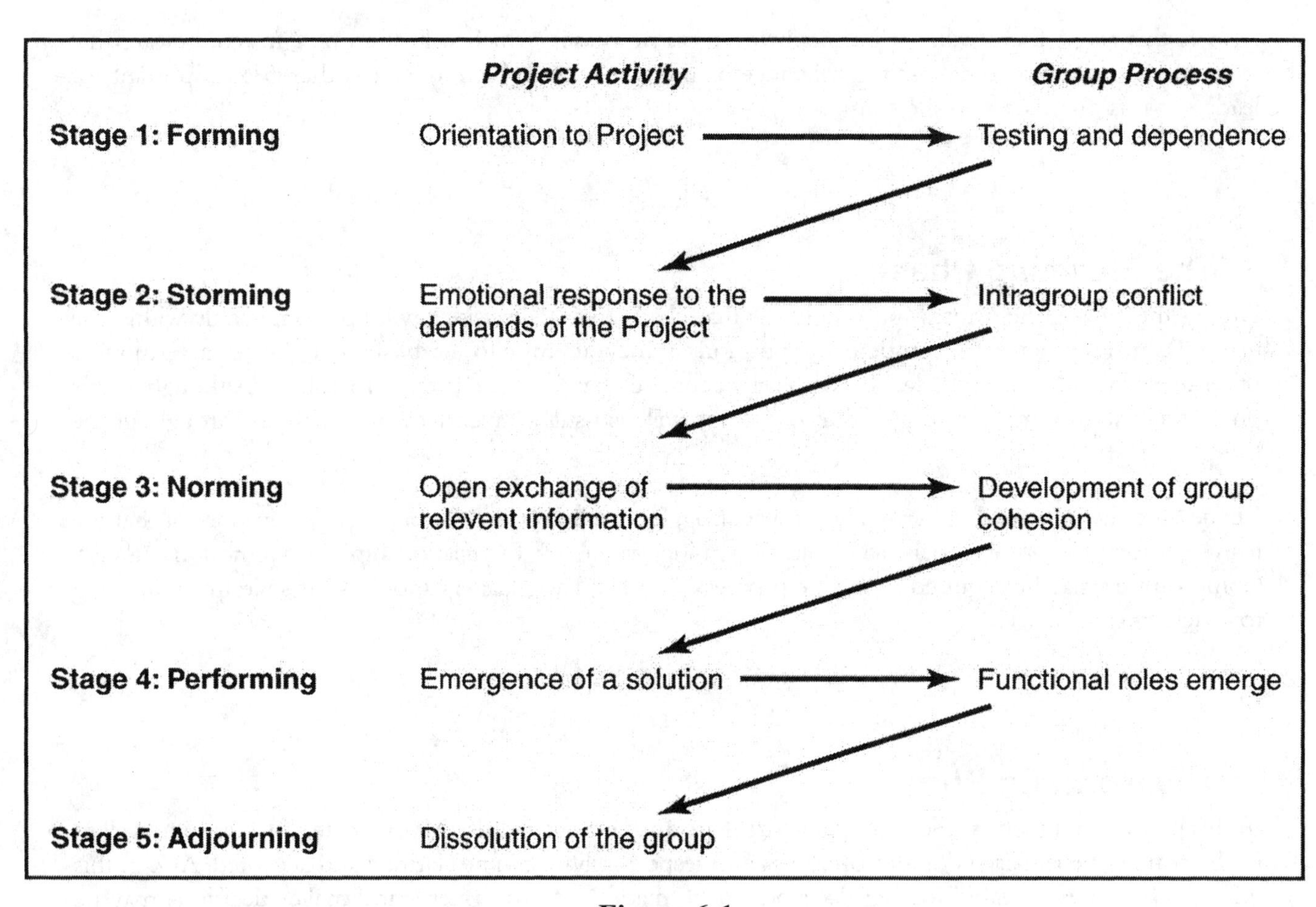
Project Activity
Group Process
Stage 1: Forming
Orientation to Project
Testing and dependence
Stage 2: Storming
Emotional response to the demands of the Project
Intragroup conflict
Stage 3: Norming
Open exchange of relevent information
Development of group cohesion
Stage 4: Performing
Emergence of a solution
Functional roles emerge
Stage 5: Adjourning
Dissolution of the group

Figure 6.1

The Performing Phase

In this phase the team is more strategically aware and knows clearly why it is doing what it is doing, for good or bad. The team has a shared vision and is able to stand on its own feet with no interference or participation from the leader. Another characteristic is the present focus on over-achieving goals, with the team making most decisions against criteria agreed upon with the leader. The team also has a high degree of autonomy. Disagreements occur, but team members are now able to resolve them within the team in very positive ways, without the need for process changes.

The team at this phase is also able to work towards achieving established goals, and tend to develop relationships, style, and process along the way. The team members tend to look after each other. While the team requires delegated tasks and projects from the leader, it does not need to be instructed or assisted, although team members might ask for assistance from the leader in regards to personal and interpersonal development. In this phase, leaders delegate and oversee.

The Adjourning Phase

As mentioned earlier, in 1975 Tuckman added a fifth stage to this team-building model, the Adjourning Phase, which is also referred to as Deforming and Mourning. This last phase is arguably more of an adjunct to the original four-stage model rather than an extension, as it views the group from a perspective beyond the purpose of the first four stages. The adjourning phase is certainly very relevant to the people in the group and their well-being, but not to the main task of managing and developing a team, which is clearly central to the original four stages.

The adjourning phase is the break-up of the group, when hopefully everyone can move on to new projects. But from an organizational perspective, recognition of and sensitivity to people's vulnerabilities is helpful in this phase, especially if members of the group have been closely bonded and feel a sense of insecurity or threat from this change. Feelings of insecurity would be natural for people with high 'steadiness' attributes, and with strong routine and empathy style.

The Punctuated Equilibrium Model

It is important to note that, according to the group development Punctuated Equilibrium Model proposed by Gersick, which is depicted in figure 6.2, the team-building process is somewhat different to what Tuckman proposed. Although some experts would view these models as competing alternatives, I hold that we can take advantage of both of them simultaneously by recognizing the strengths of each.

Figure 6.2 – The Punctuated Equilibrium Model

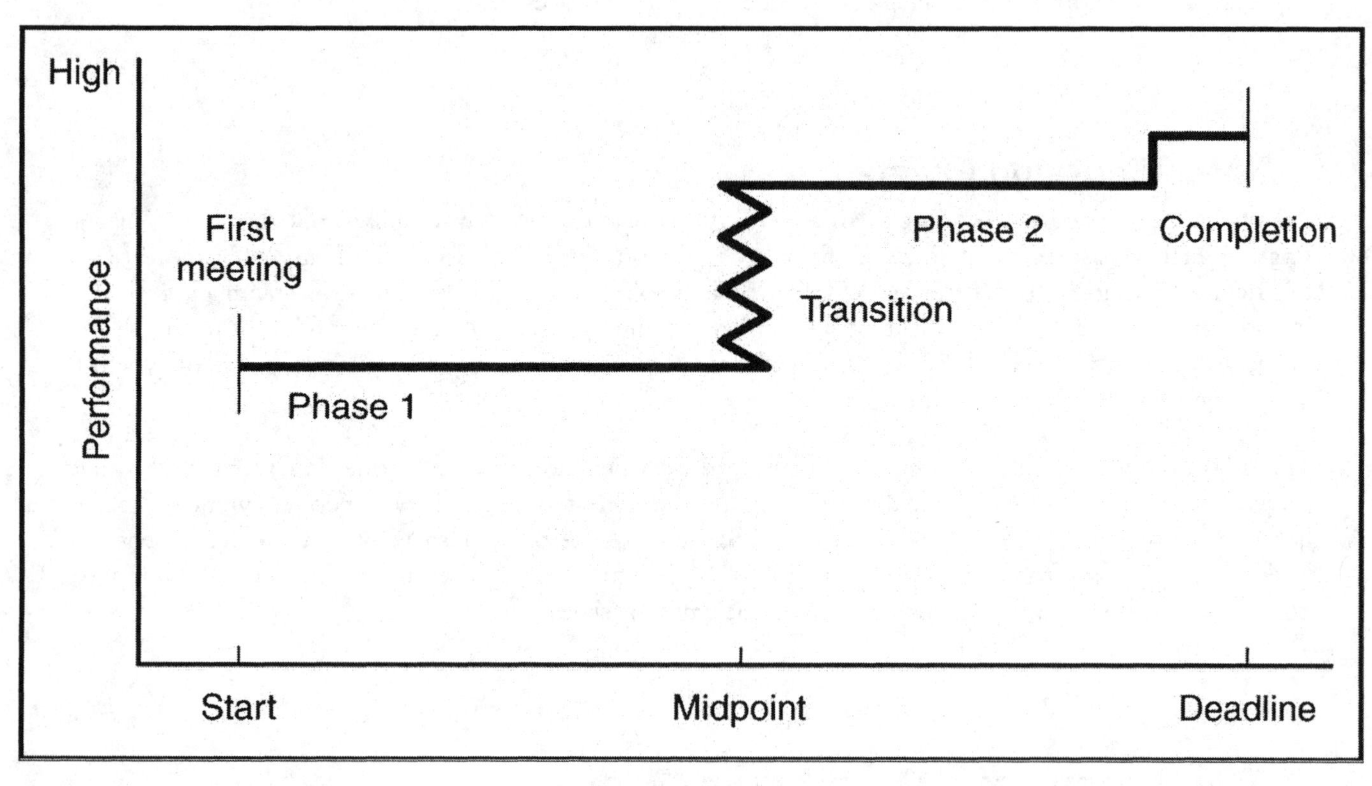
High
Performance
First
meeting
Phase 1
Transition
Phase 2
Completion
Start
Midpoint
Deadline

Figure 6.2

Gersick's model consists of six different stages of a group's processes:

1. The first stage is the direction set by the group's first meeting. This first meeting covers a framework of the group's direction, using goals and assumptions of not only the work to be done, but of the people as well.

2. Group members feel they have so much time to complete the project that they relax and socialize. This 2nd stage of group activity is one of inertia.

3. The transition phase, the third, comes at the halfway point of the completion date. A feeling of a "mid-life crisis" is felt. A sense of urgency appears. Problems are confronted. Criticism begins to be taken seriously.

4. Stage four is characterized by initiating the changes developed during the transition, dropping old patterns, and adopting new perspectives; the group sets new directions for their goals.

5. The fifth stage is once again characterized by inertia.

6. Finally, the last stage of the Punctuated-Equilibrium Model is characterized by accelerated activity. Team members or individuals realize the project is due very soon so they put forth a final burst of energy to complete their tasks, with most of the activity occurring during the last meeting.

Challenges in Building Teams

Despite the well-structured process of building teams development by Tuckman, Murphy's Law will tell you that whatever can go wrong will go wrong. So there will be plenty of challenges in building teams. In coping with those challenges it is very important that team leaders devise ways to prevent and mitigate these challenges. The list below is not exhaustive by any means, but points to areas you should be aware of, which will help in dealing with team-building challenges:[1]

- **Building team identity** - When a team is first formed, it needs to get a sense of why it is a team. Each team member must also build his or her own individual identity within the team. Each member needs to be able to answer these questions confidently:
    - Why was I chosen for this team?
    - What is my role in this team?
    - What does the team need me to achieve?
- **Establishing a climate of trust** - It is not necessary for team members to trust one another absolutely, but they must trust one another in relation to the task of the team. Facilitating and speeding up the process by which team members get to know one another helps to establish a climate of working trust.

[1] Adapted from "The Ultimate Team-Building Toolkit," by Alison Hardingham, AMACOM, 2001.

- **Dealing with conflict** - Sooner or later, every team will run into conflict. Teams that don't address conflict properly may fight a great deal or avoid the issues that cause disagreement. In contrast, the team that learns to deal with conflict effectively can solve long-lasting and widely impacting problems, and can handle any situation, irrespective of how conflict-provoking it may be.

- **Overcoming setbacks** - The commonly held belief that those who haven't failed haven't attempted anything difficult holds as true for teams as it does for individuals. Teams that perform at their potential will encounter setbacks. If the team has trouble overcoming setbacks, it will lose energy, and will not be able to analyze and learn from the failure.

- **Thinking "outside the box"** - The need to be unusually creative will arise at some time for many teams. Teams must learn to identify when "outside the box" thinking is truly necessary and learn how to accomplish it.

- **Managing change** - When change occurs, communications must occur that lets everyone know what is changing, why, when and how. Processes may need to change, goals may need to be adjusted, and the team environment may be the best context to provide emotional support to those experiencing pain associated with the change.

- **Managing complexity** - Complexity is the number and nature of reporting relationships, interconnectedness between projects, the degree of uncertainty and fluidity in task requirements, and the intricacy of critical paths leading to task achievement. Teams that manage complexity correctly focus on the right things at the right time, communicate and coordinate, plan together, and constantly clarify the roles, responsibilities, and mutual requirements one team member has in relation to another. Doing this allows a team to monitor progress and identify problems early.

- **Ensuring cabinet responsibility** - When a contentious issue arises, a decision that is made in a way that guarantees that all team members will stick to what is decided will raise the confidence and capability of a team.

- **Raising team profile** - Sometimes it is not enough for a team to simply achieve its own task goals. It may need to - and the organization may need it to - raise its profile as a team. Failing to do so may lead to team members feeling they have let themselves down and missed an opportunity to use their influence. However, if a team can meet this challenge, the organization will derive added benefit from its success.

Mastering People Management

An unexplored yet critical side of leading teams is upward leadership, or getting results by helping to guide your team leader. Rather than undermining authority or seizing power from superiors, upward leadership means stepping in when senior managers need help and support in a way that benefits everyone.

Leading up is a matter of offering a superior your strategic insights or persuading a boss to change directions before it is too late. It requires an ability to work in two directions at once, of stepping into the breach when nobody above you is doing so - and of listening to those below you before you step off a cliff yourself.

The Ups and Downs of Leading People

Upward leadership is not always welcomed. Many team leaders and managers in general have worked for a supervisor who ran the office with a fine level of detail or misjudged the future. To come forward when a superior does not encourage it can be risky but if the upward leadership works - whether welcomed or not - it can help transform decline into growth and, occasionally, turn disaster into triumph.

Upward leadership, as brilliantly discussed by Michael Useem in his book, *Leading Up*[2], is not a natural skill but it can be mastered and there are few better ways to appreciate its exercise than to study those who have had to apply it. Watching their efforts can provide lessons for leading up when it really counts.

Bold Subordinates

A few years ago, then-U.S. vice president Al Gore defeated Bill Bradley in the campaign for the Democratic presidential nomination. Many factors contributed to the defeat but among them was Bradley's reluctance to reply to stinging attacks by his opponent. His instinct had been to run his campaign above the fray - less as "a 21st-century politician," said *The New York Times*, "than as an Old Testament prophet." [3]

Although his campaign suffered defeat after defeat in the early stages, Bradley might have recovered his momentum had he hit back hard. To do that, though, the candidate needed to be led into the fray, a form of leading up that no one working for him proved willing to risk.

Bradley tended to take his own counsel more than that of campaign advisers. For their part, they did not always say what he needed to hear. An aide summed up the problem just after Bradley withdrew from the campaign in March following defeats in two states: "These people were always concerned about what their relationship with Bill should be, as opposed to just doing what it takes to win."

The apparent inability of Bradley's staff to distinguish between leading up and currying favor may have contributed to the aspirant's decline. However, the cause goes back to the man who had created such a mindset in the first place. Had Bradley pressed those who worked for him to do their best by him, even if it meant voicing criticism, they might have bolstered his run for the party's nomination.

Leading up can require fortitude and perseverance. Managers might fear how superiors will respond and doubt their right to lead up, but all carry a responsibility to do what they can when it will make a difference, and to tell a superior what he or she ought to hear. Many strategies and more than a few

---

[2] Useem, M. (2002) *Leading Up: How to Lead Your Boss So You Both Win*, American Library Association. Portions of this chapter were written by Michael Useem, who kindly contributed to this book. Mr. Useem is a professor at the Wharton School of the University of Pennsylvania and director of its Center for Leadership and Change.
[3] New York Times of March 8, 2000, "Bradley's Fatal Mistakes," by James Dao and Nicholas Kristof

organizations have failed when the middle ranks could see the problems but hesitated to challenge their command.

From the other point of view, there is also an obligation on managers to encourage people below to speak up and tell them what they need to know, to fill in for their shortcomings when future success is threatened.

A culture of upward leadership is built, not born. For that, managers should regularly insist that more junior staff examine proposals and challenge errors. Asking those of lesser rank to say what they candidly think and complimenting them for doing so are among the small measures that can make for a big improvement in attitude.

Risk and Reward[4]

Some individuals begin with a head start but everybody can improve their ability for upward service. Back in 1997, David Pottruck, COO of broker Charles Schwab, was already facing a critical decision in his career, in which the outcome depended greatly on his upward leadership skills. Could he convince his chief executive and company directors to make a radical move into internet-based client trading? It would be expensive and risky but it could also be highly advantageous.

Founded in 1974, Schwab's annual revenue had already exceeded $2 billion by 1997. Through its thousands of customer service representatives, the company bought and sold shares for a million clients and in the astounding bull market of the 1990s everyone seemed to benefit. The rise of the internet, however, threatened to undo all that, undermining a rich network of relationships painstakingly assembled over many years. The web furnished free and fast access to company information that had long been the brokers' province and it opened a way to trade stock at a fraction of the time and cost required to call a broker.

For those willing to forgo personal contact, Schwab had built an electronic trading service, charging just $29 a trade. Many customers, however, still wanted real dialogue with real people and it was from these people that the serious money came - as much as $80 a transaction. For how long, though, would these clients continue to pay $80 when they knew other clients were trading for just $29?

One solution would be to bundle full-service and online trading into one offering and so give all customers the combination that many increasingly wanted. In the spring of 1997, Pottruck decided that the two-tier system had to go, even though he was personally responsible for building much of it. In its place, he would create a single full-service offering with internet trading and he reasoned that it could cost no more than $29 a trade.

---

[4] Excerpt from Michael Useem, "The Ups and Downs of Leading People," *Financial Times*, Mastering People Management, October 29, 2001. Used with permission of the author.

Pottruck turned to his boss, Charles Schwab, for approval. Charles Schwab had already embraced the internet. He had appreciated the power of the web early and had pushed the company to move online in 1995. The founder was known to have a feel for market trends and as Pottruck explained his thinking, Charles Schwab immediately affirmed his interest in the proposed move. However, he also posed hard questions: how much would it cost, how would it affect the organization and how soon could benefits be expected? Charles Schwab was willing to take large risks and place big bets when the odds were known, and he pressed Pottruck to nail them down.

Pottruck instructed his staff to assess the effect of slashing the full service commission of $80 and providing full service to everybody at $29 a trade, including 1.2 million customers using the limited-service internet option. The strategists came back with a shocking conclusion. If the company allowed account holders to migrate, it would depress the company's revenue in 1998 by $125 million and its earnings by $100 million, more than a fifth of its projected pre-tax profits. Stock markets would be likely to drive down Schwab's share price with a vengeance.

Although he was sure of the long-term chances of the new offering, Pottruck was less sure if returns would arrive quickly enough to avert financial disaster. The plan would require vigorous support from the chief executive and board members if it were to succeed. Pottruck himself was in the best position to make the case.

He gave Charles Schwab the financial implications of the low-price full service and warned of the effect on profits in the short term. Following weeks of discussion, Schwab endorsed the plan. The founder always insisted on putting customer service first and Pottruck had made that his guiding principle; Schwab had consistently stressed careful analysis, which Pottruck had done; Schwab had delegated much to those he trusted and Pottruck had already earned his confidence.

The next stop for Pottruck was the company directors, without whose wholehearted approval it would be foolish to proceed. Pottruck brought his plan to the board in September 1997. Some directors wondered why any change was needed since the year was already proving to be the best in company history. After-tax profits were approaching $270 million, and what Pottruck was now proposing would slash them by a third or more. Others wondered if the options had been thoroughly studied. Still others asked if the downside could be weathered. Pottruck's confident response was: "It will be fine but it will take some time", possibly a year and a half or more. The directors duly agreed on what would be the company's most fateful decision of the era. On January 15 1998, Schwab announced it was offering web trading for $29 a time and was extending all services to all customers - consultations at branches and by telephone, and personal advice.

The first quarter's results - as Pottruck had forecast - were devastated. Schwab was indeed cannibalizing its full-service, high-priced accounts. Quarterly revenues had been growing at 6.5 percent per quarter in 1997; now they declined by 3 percent.

Pre-tax income had been rising by 8 percent per quarter in 1997; now it dropped by 16 percent.

Yet the expectation that the world was moving to the web proved prescient. By the end of 1998, the number of Schwab customers with online accounts nearly doubled and Schwab finished the year with 20 percent growth in revenue and 29 percent rise in profit.

Meeting the internet challenge at Schwab required keen insight and a reasoned capacity to risk much when others doubted the proposed path. It also depended on a boss ready to be persuaded and a board ready to be moved. However, that readiness was not automatic. Rather, it was the product of steps that Pottruck had earlier taken to establish a relationship of confidence with those above him.

Learning to lead up is a lifelong endeavor and it is greatly helped by a willingness to learn from past mistakes and superiors who are willing to suggest how it is done.

Taking risks is a defining element of any leadership and calculated management of risk is essential. To succeed as a risk-taker on behalf of superiors, decisions need to be taken quickly and accurately. In spite of the uncertainties and large stakes that may be involved, if decisions are for managers to take, it is essential for them to do so rather than kick the responsibility upstairs.

The first step in winning the support of superiors and the board is ensuring accuracy. The second is to communicate carefully why the proposed course of action is necessary and how it can be accomplished with the minimum upheaval.

The Cost of Failure

When organizations foster upward leadership, the benefits can be great. Conversely, the costs of ignoring or discouraging it can be enormous. Consider a recent example.

In February of 2001, the nuclear submarine USS Greenville suddenly surfaced and collided with a Japanese fishing boat, the Ehime Maru. The boat overturned and nine passengers were killed. A navy investigator reported that a visiting officer on the Greenville had sensed that Commander Scott D. Waddle[5] was rushing preparations and cutting corners to give a demonstration to 16 civilians on board - but the visiting officer had said nothing to the commander about his concerns.

Similarly, Waddle's second-ranking officer, who carried the most explicit obligation to challenge questionable procedures, had failed to voice his own doubts about his commander's pace, including an abbreviated periscope inspection of the horizon just before the surfacing. The subordinate officer, the investigator found, "was thinking these things, but did not articulate them to the commanding officer."

The investigator concluded that the crew members so respected their captain that they were reluctant to challenge him. Commanding officer Waddle, he found, "doesn't get a lot of corrective input from

[5] According to article entitled "Sub Commander Reprimanded," *The Washington Post*, April 24, 2001.

subordinates because he's very busy giving directions, and the ship has experienced a lot of success when he does." Had the institution more effectively stressed its principle of upward challenge, had the visiting officer and the commander's subordinates been emboldened to question their commander's actions, the fatal event may have never happened.

Even short of the loss of life, the cost of failure for upward leadership can be huge. Consider the price of such an error for the chairman of Samsung Group, Lee Kun Hee. In 1994, he decreed that Samsung should invest $13 billion to become a car producer, aiming to make 1.5 million vehicles by 2010. Car manufacture was already a crowded field, plagued by global over-capacity, but Lee was a powerful chieftain and a passionate car buff, and none of his subordinates questioned his strategy.

A year after the first cars rolled off the line in 1999, however, Samsung Motors sold its assets to Renault. Many of Samsung's top managers had silently opposed the investment, and Lee later told them he was puzzled why none had openly expressed their reservations. By then, though, Lee had reached into his own pocket for $2 billion to placate his irate creditors.

Courage to Lead Up

A common element among those who successfully lead up is a driving urge to make things happen on high, an unflinching willingness to take charge when not fully in command. The exercise of upward leadership has been made easier by contemporary expectations in many companies that managers learn not just from their superiors but from all points of the compass. The phrase "360-degree feedback" has come to mean a manager's annual task of gathering reaction from direct subordinates and immediate bosses. So it is with leading up: instead of just motivating those below, managers must also muster those above; instead of just learning from those above, managers need listen to those below.

Such leadership can be inspired when executives are willing to take the time to create the right culture. Once established, a company-wide emphasis on leading upwards serves as a kind of inertial guidance system, continually reminding everybody that they are obliged to stand up without the need for superiors to ask for them to do so. Figure 6.3 provides some of the cornerstone principles for team members and corporate managers in leading up.

Figure 6.3 - Principles of leading up for KM managers

Figure 6.4 provides some of the cornerstone principles for chief "x" officers (in particular CEOs and CKOs) in leading up, as these upper managers are many times key in building their corporate team.

Figure 6.4 - Principles of leading up for Chief "x" Officers

Leading Up Principles

- ✓ Building superiors' confidence in you requires giving them your confidence.
- ✓ The bond between manager and executive should be a relationship based on an open flow of information and respect.
- ✓ The more uncertain or irresolute your superiors are about achieving a goal, the more clear-minded and determined you must be in formulating and executing your strategy.
- ✓ If your superiors do not appreciate a grave threat, transcend the normal channels of communication to drive home the message.
- ✓ Persistence often pays but it requires determination to stay on a rocky path when you have persuaded those above and below you to follow.
- ✓ However hostile your superior, however harsh your message, the well being of those in your hands must remain foremost.

Figure 6.3

Leading Up Principles for Chief "x" Officers

- ✓ If you want subordinates to offer their best advice, you must value and make use of it.
- ✓ Stay tuned to what your subordinates are implying or communicating through other means. Because their personal stake in you and the company is large, they may appreciate your situation better than you do yourself.
- ✓ If you expect those below to support your leadership and step into the breach when needed, they will need to understand your strategy, methods and rules. That requires repeated restatements of your principles and consistent adherence to them.
- ✓ Downward leadership and upward leadership reinforce one another; if you are effective at the former, it will encourage the latter; if you are adept at the latter, it can inspire the former.

Figure 6.4

In addition to leading up, two leadership qualities should also be apparent in every team leader: builders and strategists. So if you want to be a successful team builder you must be a self-starter who is excited by business development and by growing your team. A critical attribute of such entrepreneurship is being a strategist who can grapple with the implications of using team building as a tool for corporate transformation.

To a degree, as discussed earlier in this chapter, by being a team builder you should also be a visionary, able to see the big picture that the upper management has in mind, but also able to translate it into action, to think of new ways of doing things and yet focus on deliverable results. Team leaders (and builders!) are, therefore, entrepreneurs inside organizations. However, vision and determination are not enough. Team builders are also consultants, bringing in ideas and listening to other people's ideas, and backing them if they make sense and fit the knowledge vision.

Chapter 7
Valuing Team Diversity

***There is only one truth, steadfast, healing, salutary, and that is the absurd.*[1]**

We all would like to think that building a team is essentially a rational exercise, that it works like any other tangible interaction in this world, and that we should therefore be able to gain from it, as it works to our benefit. However, we just need to look at the financial section of any newspaper, the TV news, the financial bulletins, at the *Wall Street Journal*, to realize that businesses (nothing more than a bunch of teams working together), particularly in the 21st century, are anything but rational.

This chapter discusses exactly that, the leader's dilemma in making sense out of something that makes no sense at all: the diversity within any team. In having to rely on their instincts as the only tangible source of information to address these gaps, the challenges of team-building strategies and practices, team builders are more than ever before faced with the imperative need to understand what I call the *science of bridging the gap*. In other words, to understand how the way they think shapes what they see, and how paradox and absurdity inevitably play a major part in their every action.

Managing Team-Building Chaos: A Sea of Gaps

In order to innovate and effectively compete in the knowledge economy, "learning" teams must become "knowing" teams. They must rely on the team's instinct and tap into their collective wisdom. The bottom line is, every team has collective wisdom and instinct, which propels the generation of "gaps" between what is known (explicit) and what is somewhat known (tacit). Teams should always strive to generate as many gaps as possible. After all, gaps are the seeds of innovation. But by the same token, teams must bridge such gaps as quickly as possible; otherwise chaos emerges.

Poor working relationships among team members, internal and external strife, conflicts, misunderstandings, low productivity, decreased customer satisfaction, lack of referrals, poor communication, and low sales are all symptoms of chaos within the teams of an organization (as well as its partners and distribution channels). These are all symptoms of gaps that are not being bridged, be it intentionally or not. This knowledge economy we are in is characterized by constant and fast changes, and to be successful, teams and team members must embrace change as quick as it comes. In other words, this level of diversity within teams (and outside!) must be valued, instead of opposed. We tend to

---

[1] Andrew Salmon

want to homogenize human relations, business processes and teams. We must resist this temptation if we want to build successful teams

Nonetheless, to prevent chaos, or a proliferation of gaps, team leaders must embody the science of bridging gaps, of dealing with ever-changing environments and business landscapes, by developing a productive, team-oriented, positive atmosphere where good communication is paramount. In the 21st century economy, team leaders, and the team as a whole, must learn not only to manage time, but also to manage themselves. Rather than focus on tasks and time, leaders must focus on preserving and enhancing relationships inside the teams, and on accomplishing results.

The reality is, there will always be more to do than can be done by one person. If you are only doing the work of two people, you are loafing in your company. It doesn't matter whether it is two full-time jobs, four or twelve that you have to do. Your team's productivity is the result of the trust the members of the team have on each other. If you have the right trust, working relationship and environment, the work gets done!

As a lecturer at Boston University's[2] (BU) graduate program, I have the opportunity to interact with management and computer sciences students. I'm pleased to recognize that, unlike many other programs in management at other universities and colleges today, BU's program is keen on educating management professionals not to take for granted the complexity and paradoxical nature of human teams. In my own lectures I'm quick to point out that thinking loses out to how-to formulas, which is one of the issues the Knowledge Tornado[3] concept deals with, turning know-how into how-to, knowledge into action. Considering the task-oriented nature of MBA candidates, it is not surprising that these students, as well as the majority of business managers and executives, still find themselves prone to accept a definition of management that makes it seem as if it could be simply learned.

Chaos, the end-result of gaps, is a wonderfully evocative word, a formless void of primordial matter, the great deep or, if you prefer, the abyss out of which the cosmos or order of the universe was evolved. Can you think of anything better calculated to set the creative energies of executives (team leaders!) in motion than the challenge of forming order from the chaos-imminent changes in their business and team?

A challenge, a gap, it certainly is. Many management and technology icons have responded to it and made remarkable progress in the last few years, but much remains to be done. The word on the street was that MBAs and other advanced management studies were redundant, that anyone could be a CEO and successfully run a company. Since the burst of the dot-com bubble that opinion is not encountered as often. Seemingly overnight, executives learned that, in the business world, especially one characterized by virtual enterprises and goods sold, executives, in particular CEO's, must also be information professionals. As such, the ability to build a meaningful business within the void is being increasingly valued.

One of the most important lessons the dot-com era taught executives was that you do not build a company in five days; you don't do an IPO in a couple of months. For those companies that survived the first impact of the stock market crash in 2000, it was very hard initially to know how to break through the chaos barrier, as shown in figure 7.1, which depicts the stages of a knowledge tornado. Where could they begin? Savvy and successful executives answered by taking one first small step: developing a business

---

[2] At the Metropolitan College

[3] For more information, please read *The Knowledge Tornado: Bridging the Corporate Knowledge Gap,* by Marcus Goncalves, 2002

virtual enterprises and goods sold, executives, in particular CEO's, must also be information professionals. As such, the ability to build a meaningful business within the void is being increasingly valued.

One of the most important lessons the dot-com era taught executives was that you do not build a company in five days; you don't do an IPO in a couple of months. For those companies that survived the first impact of the stock market crash in 2000, it was very hard initially to know how to break through the chaos barrier, as shown in figure 7.1, which depicts the stages of a knowledge tornado. Where could they begin? Savvy and successful executives answered by taking one first small step: developing a business strategy for what they would want to collect and preserve from their business, a laser-beam focus approach - if only they could find the wherewithal to do so!

Figure 7.1 – The knowledge tornado concept

You see, there was no corporate memory that could lead them into the right direction and, sadly, most of them did not know or rely on their corporate instinct. Thus they started on a long, steep learning curve. As of spring 2006, the great majority of the dot-com corporations that survived (98% of them died[4]) are still spinning, burning cash and trying to figure out where to go next. Take a look at Wall Street and you will find that companies like CMGI, Internet Capital Group, Mercator and many others have already disappeared, while many others still do not have a clear perspective of where to go next. That is, they are still in the gap, in the chasm I should say, enduring their everyday chaos, waiting for a clear strategy to surface. If it ever does.

Unfortunately, schools are not teaching managers to lead their team through gaps, never mind bridge them when they occur. While businesses are booming everything is great, but when a hiccup in the economy happens, then it is doomsday. The problem is, managers (leaders!), particularly in the US and other developed countries, have been accustomed to believe the familiar bromides. When a manager, or any leader or executive, believes that their responsibilities can be discharged adequately by attending seminars or following simplistic formulas, then we have a problem. When such formulas fail them, not only do they get discouraged and frustrated, but also sometimes they totally derail.

What is it about the 21st century economy that feels so chaotic to team leaders? Is it the sheer volume of information that needs to be absorbed? Is it the lack of quality assurance we have been used to in financial literature and media? Is it the uncertainty about the authority of many business concepts and theories – mine included? Is it not knowing what is out there, especially beyond our international borders? Is it the unmanageable number of materials, experts, gurus and consulting practices you encounter when attempting to seek advice out professional service? Could it be the actual lack of expertise in the industry? Or, could it be the difficulty of establishing a business strategy, a business goal, one that you are sure you won't get you fired by the Board? Perhaps it is the ephemeral nature of being a leader in the 21st century: Here today, but changed or gone tomorrow.

---

[4] According to ARC Advisory Groups' report (www.arcweb.com)

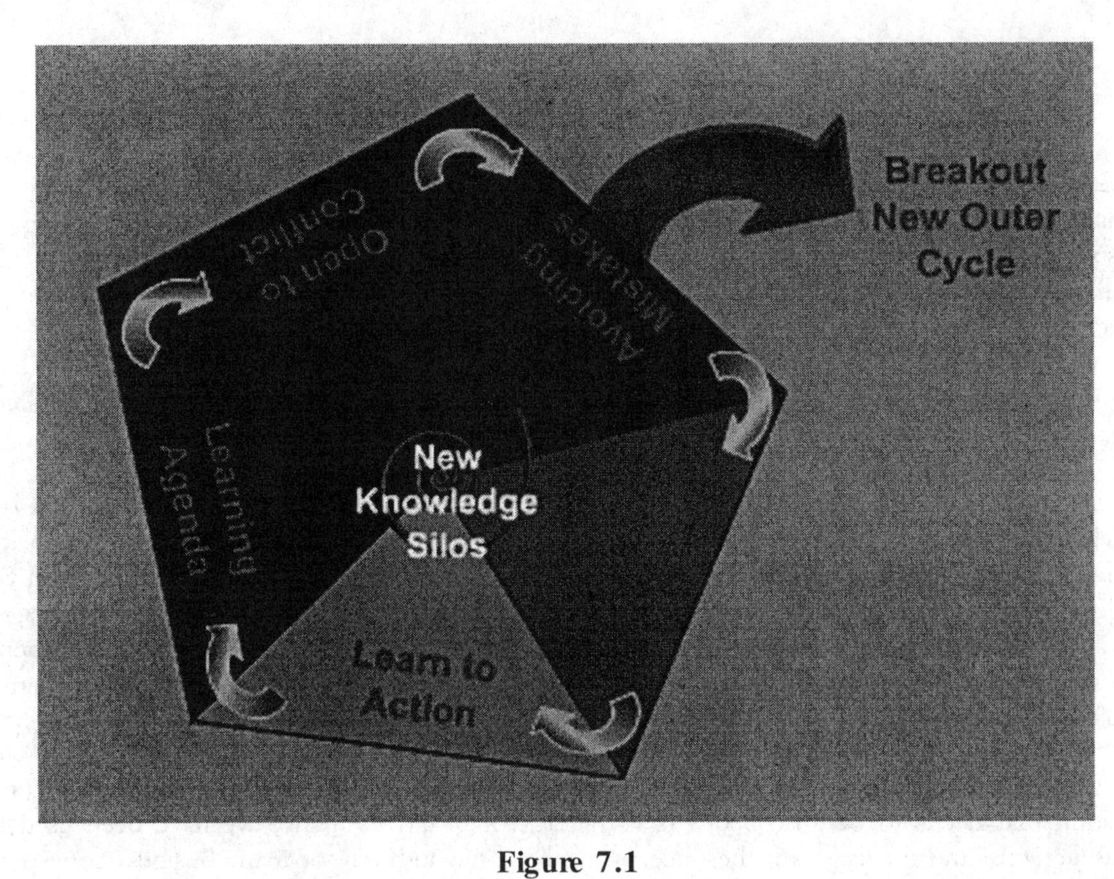
Breakout
New Outer
Cycle
Open to
Conflict
Avoiding
Mistakes
Learning
Agenda
New
Knowledge
Silos
Learn to
Action

Figure 7.1

Complexity science suggests that paradoxes are not problematic. Rather, they create a tension from which creative solutions emerge. This realization can shake someone at the core of his being. Charles Handy[6], for example, writes that "the important message for me was that there are never any simple or right answers in any part of life. I used to think that there were, or could be. I now see paradoxes everywhere I look. Every coin, I now realize, has at least two sides." Others see the concept of paradox as so important that they now define leadership as essentially the management of paradoxes. Paradoxes are defined as simultaneous or interdependent opposites.

The Value of Diversity: What Bridges a Gap is a New Gap

Rational and logical thinking has been responsible for most achievements in life. However, as these achievements were archived and access to them became possible, answers to previously unknown problems became searchable, thus limiting and constricting our ability to think creatively, to innovate. Just think about the automobile industry. Nothing has really changed, except for the first forays into hybrid cars, since the invention of automobile. Cars are still running on wheels and burning fossil fuel. Yet, from the invention of the wheel to cars pushed by horses, steam cars and finally the first engine-propelled car, not many years had gone by. Yet each of those stages transcended the next. The same holds true for architecture and building construction.

I believe the problem is that we have grown unsecured. Unfortunately, the price of relief from anxiety is the loss of creative ability. This is surely why we lost innovative teachers, who felt there was no room for creativity, with the latest decade of change. At the beginning of the 20th century, inventors were bold risk-takers who had to rely a lot on their own instincts, as there was not much memory (libraries, knowledge resources) available beyond their own experimentation.

The concept of dealing with gaps didn't exist, as life itself was a big gap; no wonder there were so many schools of philosophical thought, in particular existentialism. Today's leaders, for the most part, are not willing to take risks. After all, many of them are afraid of what the Board will say, how Wall Street will judge them, what will happen if they are wrong, and so on. Instead of bridging gaps with another gap, they get immobilized. They become victims of their own contradictory impulses.

While delivering a workshop for a group of executives and senior technical managers in Brasilia, Brazil, I talked with at least three executives who clearly wanted to succeed in their business, but at the same time showed all the signals of wanting to fail as well. Everything they did carried both messages. One of them, from a major bank in Brazil, would be very excited about the prospect of automating certain decision-making process within his team. However, at the same time, all he did all day long was to cripple the project by refusing to delegate, undermining his newly formed task force committee, failing to meet deadlines, and stalling on crucial decisions.

---

6 In his book *The Age of Paradox,* Harvard Business School Press, 1994.

Contradictory impulses are present in every project, every team. Thus every situation, every outcome, every achievement, can be both good and bad. That's why the science of bridging the gaps is essentially a challenge every team builder must face; the management of dilemmas, coping with contradictions while appreciating the coexistence of opposites is crucial to the development of a different way of thinking.

All Things are Impermanent: Bridges Don't Last

It is evident that all things are impermanent, including the bridges used to overcome gaps. But didn't they use to fade, or change, more slowly? Not long ago, businesses were experiencing massive restructurings, re-engineering and redirection. Skills and tools were needed for response to various impacts, to help us create rather than react. But now we are spinning faster, and the group change tools do not always seem to work. The reason is two-fold: mistakenly identifying problems and believing once a gap is bridged it will always be bridged.

Both assumptions are incorrect. First, many executives have difficulty distinguishing a problem from a predicament. Problems can always be solved, while predicaments can only be coped with. Spending time and energy on a predicament will only bring frustration, discouragement and desolation. Most issues one faces in life, marriage, family issues, business affairs and so on, are complicated and inescapable. They tend to be predicaments in which no option is a best option, where all tend to be relative. Building teams in the 21st century is a lot like that. In this new economy, the management-information-system (MIS) team will most likely not be able to meet the needs of executive management, either because their systems will become inadequate or possibly because of the technology illiteracy of the executives.

By accepting that all things are impermanent, team builders can take advantage of business tools that help them solve problems and accept predicaments, actually taking advantage of them, as those are very possibly the only consistent data they will have. Thus some strategies to copy with the paradox of bridging gaps are outlined below.

Coping with Team Diversity: Understanding the Eye of the Tornado

Consider for a moment the outer limits of the tornado. It is chaotic, as it causes great devastation and changes everything it touches in the team. Then think of the center of the tornado, the eye. There all is calm, peaceful and quiet. Think of it as your present team status. For sure you will not be able to stop or even control the wind and the noise around the team, be it the noises of competition, shifts in market winds and so on.

When building a team it is quite similar. You can remain in the center of your own "tornado" (your status quo) and flow with the wind, with the tornado. It does seem to be the obvious thing to do. However, doing so will only postpone the inevitable: the periphery of the tornado will eventually come crashing your team down. Do you remember the movie *A Perfect Storm*? The situation encountered in the movie was not a predicament, and it had a solution. But the solution required courage and the willingness to fail and die, crash and burn, as the fishermen did. But a calculated and well-thought out strategy, one that transcends the team's memory and taps into the team's instinct, enables you to traverse the walls of the tornado. Keep in mind that doing little other than that which seems absolutely safe runs a much bigger risk than taking a chance. Risks are how we learn from our successes (not mistakes!).

Know What Matters

Michael Korda[7], the novelist, once said that "the first rule of success, and the one that supersedes all others, is to have energy. It is important to know how to concentrate it and focus it on the important things, instead of frittering it away on trivia." The most powerful thing you can do at any moment is re-focus. Ask yourself: What do you want to achieve? Why is this important?

Keep in mind that gaps are inevitable; you will always have to deal with the consequences of changes in any team you build. And the fact that your team is learning only makes the advent of changes even more inevitable, as awareness is part of the process. Once you learn that there is no face lost in abandoning all hope of avoiding gaps, you can get down to the task of managing how to decide which bits of it are worthy of your attention and, more importantly, which are not.

Your goal should always be bridging the gap, continuing to build the team, which is the same as transcending, not adapting the team. Many people come to this epiphany when they have their second child. All the angst spent worrying about potential crises with the first child turns into considered risk management. With the first one it's *"Oh my God - keep him away from that - it's got dirt on it!!,"* and panic setting in. With the second one it's *"Well, it's only dirt,"* and serenity flowing. Once you learn that gaps are part of building teams and transcending them part of the drill, you then transform your team into a knowing team, dependent on the next gap, so you can learn one more time and set a distance from your competitors. Much like surfers, you should look at gaps as the waves, the necessary element for a fun ride, full of emotions, accomplishments and lessons learned.

The trick is to continually assess issues based on the amount of influence you have on the team you are building, and determining their outcome. If you have no influence, your worrying isn't going to help, so don't worry. If you have a moderate amount, do what you can and be satisfied that you've done your best. If you have great influence, then set it as a priority and influence away. No time to worry.

Maintain Your Network

No team is an island, and the 21st century will be characterized by partnerships and alliances. Any team operates best when interdependent. So if you are trying to build a team as you read this, it may be time to re-value partners, to re-assess alliances, to re-energize team consciousness in the workplace and community of practices. As depicted in figure 7.2, make sure to feed your team with a vision. In the process, inspire your team, have passion for the vision and for building the team. Your team members will notice it and be impacted by it. Also, make sure to communicate at all times, don't get bogged down with tactical tasks, and keep the strategic sense, the big picture, alive.

---

[7] In *Another Life,* Delta, 2000

Figure 7.2 – Requirements for an effective team vision

One of the keys for bridging gaps is the ability to tap into support facilities. Productivity almost invariably increases when it is delegated, leveraged and pulled together. Thus, maintain your network of contacts:

- Begin using a contact manager
- Keep all of your contacts – business, school, friends, acquaintances
- Be a source of referrals
- Let teams know you don't mind being referred
- Build a select distribution list of supply chain, distribution channels and partners that you want to keep posted on what you are doing

A Matter of Communication: Avoiding Predicaments

Richard Farson[8] encourages leaders to think "beyond the conventional wisdom...to understand how the ways we think shape what we see, and how paradox and absurdity inevitably play a part in our every action." According to him, we think we want creativity or change, but we really don't. We stifle creativity by playing intellectual games, judging and evaluating, dealing in absolutes, thinking stereotypically, and not trusting our own experiences (and training our employees not to trust theirs).

Nonetheless, although it is true that leadership is trapped by many paradoxes, communication can be an important vehicle in the bridging and management of gaps. Communication provides the link through which information is shared, opinions are expressed, feedback is provided and goals are formulated. Work can not be done without communication. It is necessary to communicate in order to advise, train and inform. Members of a team must translate corporate goals into action and results. In order for this to happen, all forms of correspondence must flow freely throughout the team's structure.

There is also a correlation between the willingness of every level of the team to communicate openly and frequently, and the satisfaction expressed by the workers. Most team's predicaments, from misunderstandings to disasters, from small frustrations to major morale problems, can be traced back to either a lack of communication or ineffective technique.

Communication does not take place unless there is understanding between the communicator and the audience. Simply learning to write or read or speak is not enough. Does one make music by merely striking the keys of a piano? The difference between making noise and making music is study,

---

[8] In *Managing of the Absurd: Paradox in Leadership,* Touchstone Books, 1997

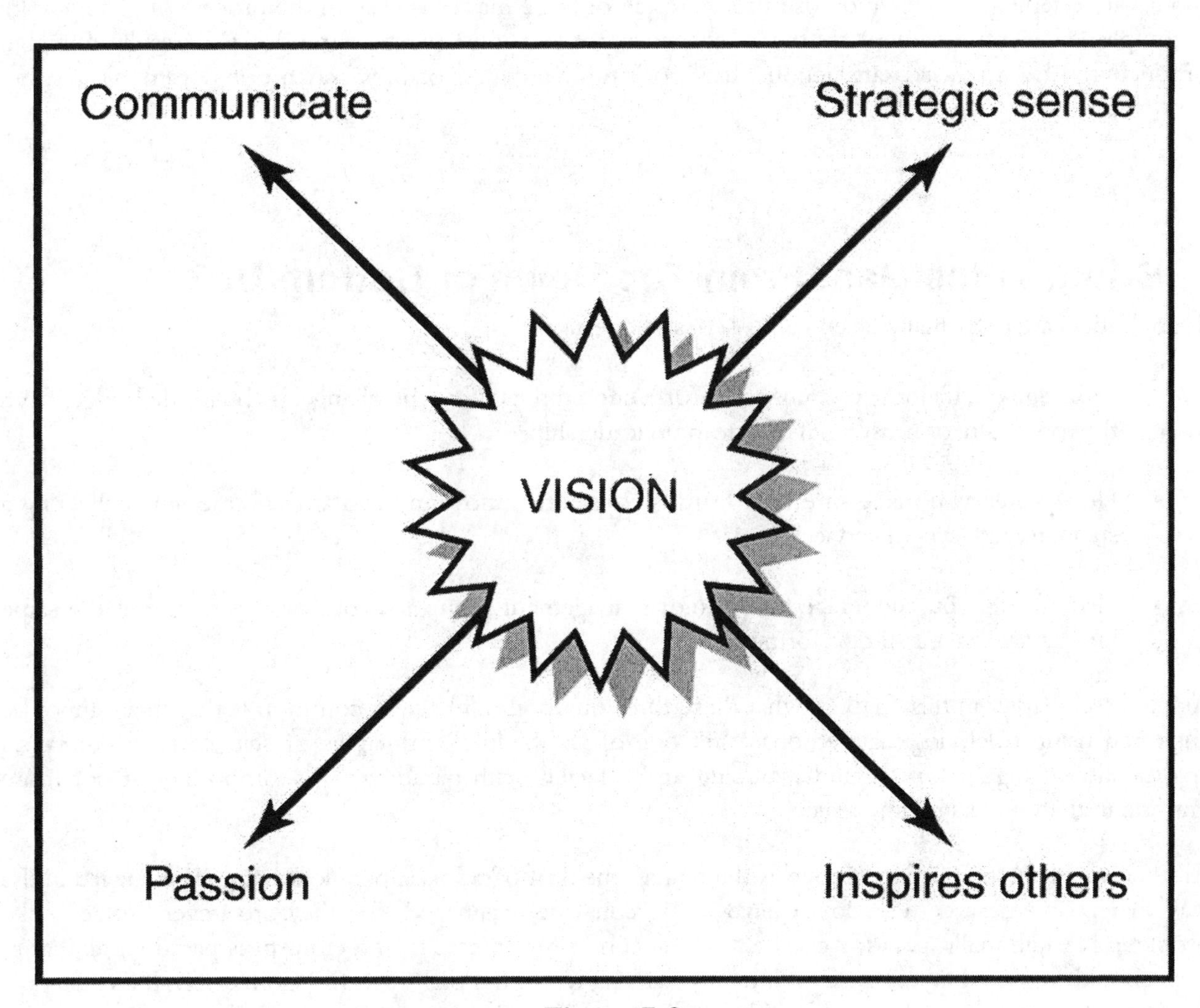
Communicate
Strategic sense
VISION
Passion
Inspires others

Figure 7.2

understanding technique, and practice, practice, practice. The same is true for communication. The difference between talking, reading, writing or hearing and communicating is study, understanding technique, and practice, practice, practice.

Therefore, team leaders should examine the process of communication within the team and strive to increase their propensity for successful communication. Messages must be clearly stated, must be brief and well-planned, and must answer the questions who, what, when, where and why.

The sending modes of communication are speaking, writing and nonverbal messages. The receiving modes are listening, reading and observation. Each of these modes is used in the process of getting work accomplished. Improvement in the effectiveness of any one of these modes will result in higher productivity and increased satisfaction. It is not simply a matter of how much one communicates, but how well.

Bridging the Gap: From Top Down or Bottom Up?

Team leaders are perpetually faced with a series of questions:

- In bridging a major gap (a change effort), should they drive the change, or build the bridge, from the top down, or must it have bottom up leadership?
- How would you make sure your team is constantly innovating and at the same time delivering a standardized level of service?
- How would you encourage your senior management group to work as a team and at the same time not lose your star performers?

As discussed earlier in this chapter, what these three questions all have in common is that they cannot be answered using solely logical methods. Yet one of the bedrock principles of science is the universal applicability of logic. But an understanding and a facility with paradoxes is as important, if not more important, than understanding logic.

Although leadership is defined above as the management of paradoxes, paradoxes are not managed in the way that problems are. Paradoxes have to be constantly managed, for they are never "solved" like problems. Additionally, paradox can be a critical concept to integrity. If a concept is paradoxical, that in itself should suggest that it smacks of integrity, which gives it the ring of truth. Conversely, if a concept is not in the least paradoxical, you should be suspicious of it and suspect that it has failed to integrate some aspect of the whole. Such a premise is very important in generating and evaluating Koulopoulos's concept of collective corporate wisdom.

Chapter 8
Self-Directed and Self-Managed Teams

Team Building is an Exercise in Leadership: Work Hard, Play Hard.

Much of the confusion about teams in the workplace has to do with loose definitions of terms. Let's start off on the right foot by specifying what a few key words and phrases mean:

- **Team** - A group of people working together toward a common goal (i.e., a soccer team)
- **Work Group** - A group of people working together (i.e., a group of people working on different tasks at a warehouse)
- **Self-Managed Team** - A group of people working together in their own way toward a common goal that is defined outside the team (i.e., MGCG's international teams; they all execute on the vision and goals we define from Boston, but the teams do their own work scheduling, training, rewards and recognition, etc.)
- **Self-Directed Team** - A group of people working together in their own way toward a common goal which the team defines (i.e., similar to above, only that the team also handles compensation and discipline, and acts as a profit center by defining its own future)

Self-Managed versus Hierarchical Teams

Before anyone would try to implement something as aggressive as a self-managed (and subsequently self-directed) team, they should know and be able to articulate the expected benefits. A mature self-managed team, when compared to typical hierarchical management, would have measured results showing:

More	Less
Enthusiasm	Individual opinion about what's important
Learning from peers	Reliance on individual abilities
Comfort knowing help is there	Panic when workload peaks
Camaraderie	Backbiting
Shared responsibility	Protecting information
Focus on the organization	What's in it for me?
Responsibility for the team	Stress on the "supervisor"
Simple, visible measurement	Feeling unaccomplished

Performance versus Building

To create a team, a demand for performance is more important than team-building exercises. You can get a group together and train them in teamwork for weeks, but they won't be a team until they have a common understanding of the need to perform. First comes the strategic plan, then the tasks needed to carry out the plan and then, finally, teams are formed to do the tasks.

If you have read thus far, you must have realized that team basics are often overlooked. When we talk about team basics, we are talking about size, purpose, goals, skills, approach and accountability. It is important to not overlook those aspects of the team, as they will impact its ability to mature in a timely fashion and to perform.

Figure 8.1 depicts the basic requirements for building a high-performance team. The task becomes more complex when building teams at the top of the corporate hierarchy, as executives have complex, long-term challenges and heavy demands on their time. Furthermore, they got where they are by pushing hard and not necessarily by working as a team. There is no need to throw out the hierarchy though, especially because, as will be discussed in chapter 9, teams are the best way to integrate across structural boundaries. They are also the best way to design and energize core processes.

Figure 8.1 – Creating a high performance team

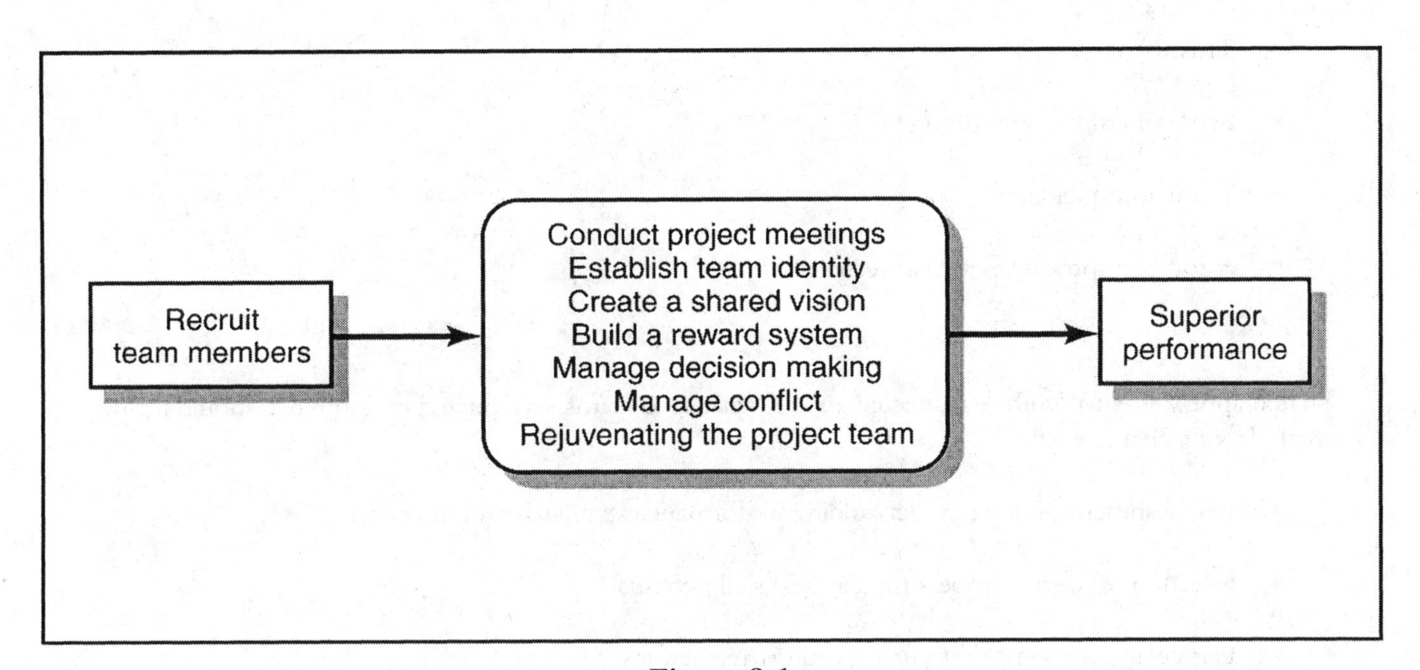
Recruit team members
Conduct project meetings
Establish team identity
Create a shared vision
Build a reward system
Manage decision making
Manage conflict
Rejuvenating the project team
Superior performance

Figure 8.1

Considerations about Self-Managed and Self-Directed Teams

The focus of self-managed teams should be to fully utilize the resources that knowledge teams bring from all functional groups. The self-directed team concept will always tend to bring greater participation, flexibility and autonomy.

The Leader's Role in a Self-Directed Team

In this model, the manager's role changes to more progressive functions such as leader, coach, assistant, expeditor, facilitator, sponsor and cheerleader. To be successful, such a team must be attentive to the following factors:

- Trustworthiness
- Sense of empowerment
- Team accountability
- A focus on process as well as results.

Shared approaches for both self-directed and self-managed teams, as depicted in figure 8.2, should include the following characteristics:

- Establishment of urgency, demanding performance standards and direction
- Selection of team members for skill and skill potential
- Particular attention paid to first meetings and actions
- Establishment of clear rules of behavior
- Establishment of immediate performance-oriented tasks and goals
- Positive feedback, recognition and reward
- Zero tolerance for negativism

Figure 8.2 – Building high performance teams, both self-directed and managed

Recruiting Project Members

- Factors affecting recruiting
  - Importance of the project
  - Management structure used to complete the project
- How to recruit?
  - Ask for volunteers
- Who to recruit?
  - Problem-solving ability
  - Availability
  - Technological expertise
  - Credibility
  - Political connections
  - Ambition, initiative, and energy

Figure 8.2

It is also very important to identifying the team's SWOT (Strengths, Weaknesses, Opportunities and Threats). Make sure to assess both the internal and external SWOT, as shown in figure 8.3, so that the probability of the team's success can be increased. Also, make sure these analyses are performed at the beginning of the team-building process, and make sure to monitor the progress and performance of the team. Discuss the results with team members openly and give them all a chance to offer feedback. The findings may be used to aid in decisions whether or not to alter the direction of the self-directed or self-managed team concept.

Figure 8.3 – SWOT analysis of teams should be performed early on in the building process, and both internally and externally

The self-directed team concept will bring greater participation, flexibility and autonomy. Major benefits would include:

- Higher qualitative results
- Increases in efficiency and productivity
- Product knowledge - ideas from a broader source are discussed while members learn more about the product/product line than they would normally
- Problem-solving skills - team members learn more from each other.
- Better decision-making - not only better, but in most cases quicker
- Improved response time.
- Shared tools/ideas - new tools/ideas are brought in by fellow team members.
- Better customer service

"Employee Empowerment" is a relatively new concept. Fear of losing control, mistrust, lack of confidence, fear of change and the inability to delegate, which typically will appear as "threats" during the SWOT analysis, must be dealt with quickly and seriously. Cross-Functional teams can remove the rigidity in thinking and let people see outside their own functional areas (avoidance of the so called Paradigm Paralysis).

Figure 8.4 depicts a SWOT analysis I conducted at a major power generation company. Notice that you can quickly identify the threats and weaknesses of the team (of about 35 members), as well as its strengths, which can lead to the development of opportunities. This particular SWOT was based on the CMMI (Capability Maturity Model Integration) model developed by the SEI (Software Engineering Institute) and the Project Management Institute's OPM3 (Organization Project Management Maturity Model).

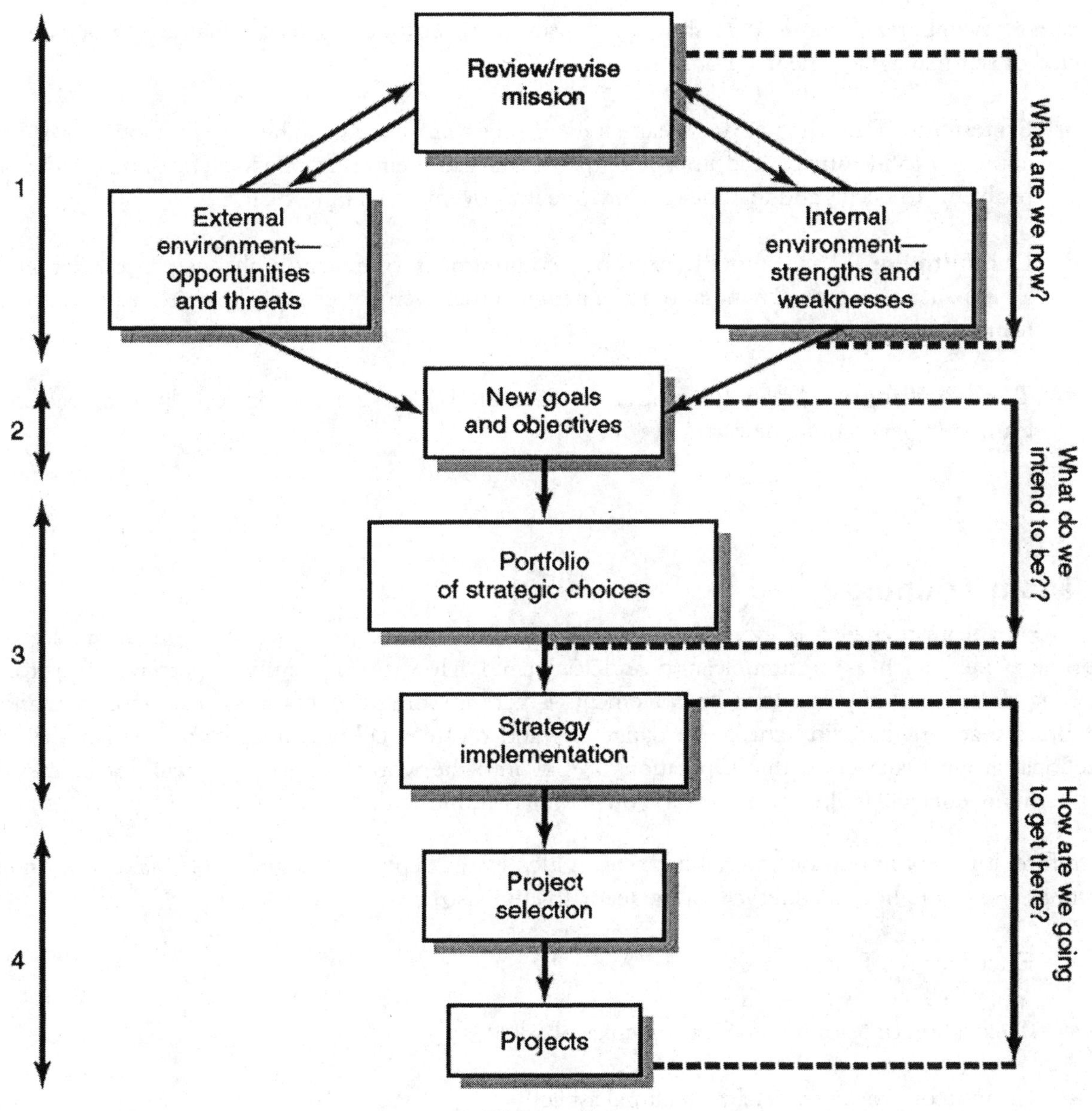
Review/revise mission
External environment—opportunities and threats
Internal environment—strengths and weaknesses
New goals and objectives
Portfolio of strategic choices
Strategy implementation
Project selection
Projects
1
2
3
4
What are we now?
What do we intend to be??
How are we going to get there?

Figure 8.3

Figure 8.4 – SWOT analysis results at a major power generation company

Leadership Pitfalls Relative to Work Teams

There are several areas team leaders should be aware of when building teams that are to become self-directed or self-managed. The main ones are:

- **Systematic Thinking** - Most team leaders today are reactive. They don't adopt a systematic approach to identifying and improving processes and their components. They normally wait for problems to occur, and then direct a process improvement team to fix it.

- **Commitment** – There should always be a commitment to the whole change process, rather than an impatience or unwillingness to make personal management changes that are required to make teams work.

- **Time & Budget** - Ability to commit the time and budget for training to help team leaders and team members acquire new skills.

Team Training

Training for team members is more than just learning the technical aspects of the job. There are other important skills, such as communication and leadership. How team members perceive their role in affecting change and implementing improvements is very important. A common response to change is caution, a reaction that can actually be dangerous and create a culture of caution. Getting the other functional group managers within Operations to buy into the work team concept will not be easy, but long-term benefits will multiply once (or if) you get full commitment..

Therefore, it is very important to establish a team identity, as depicted in figure 8.6. Make sure, in early meetings and throughout the lifecycle of the team, to emphasize:

- Effective use of meetings

- Co-location of team members as much as possible

- Creation of project team name (cultural aspect)

- Development of team rituals

Figure 8.5 – Establishing a team identity

Organizational Project Management Maturity Level

by MGCG, Inc., July 2004

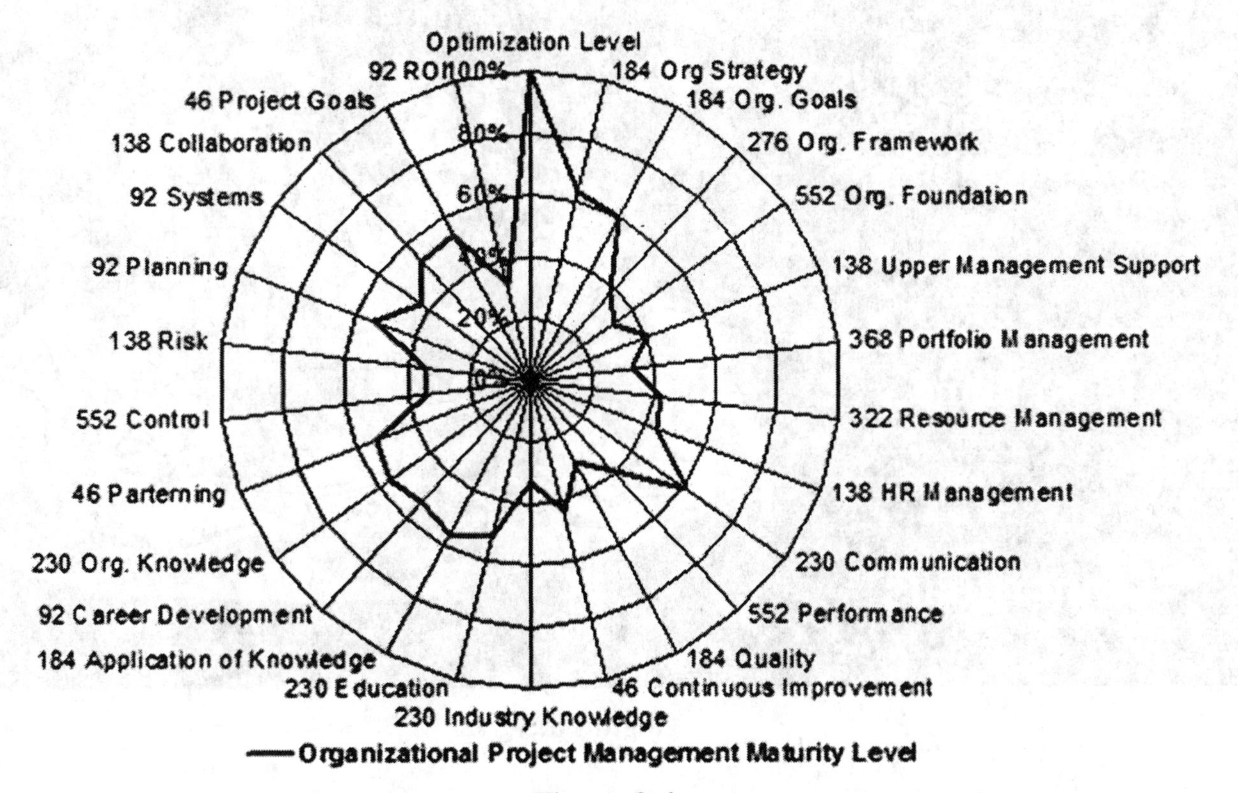

Figure 8.4

Effective Use
of Meetings
Co-location of
team members
Creation of project
team name
Team rituals

Figure 8.5

Why Self-Direction Works: A Review of Herzberg's Concepts

One of the subjects that has befuddled managers over the years is worker motivation. Team leaders and managers, as a group, tend to be uncomfortable with the human aspects of performance, preferring to concentrate on the more familiar technical matters. But one of the foremost researchers in this field, Frederick Herzberg, an industrial psychologist, has offered important information on the topic of work motivation and job enrichment that strikes at the heart of the success of self-direction concepts.

In the 1960's, Herzberg proposed that a person's needs break down into two categories: hygiene factors and motivational factors, as illustrated in figure 8.7. Hygiene factors relate to our biological needs, such as providing food, clothing, and shelter. Herzberg says we have a built-in drive to avoid pain relative to these needs, so we do what is necessary, such as work, to provide what we need. Motivational factors, however, are very different. These factors include achievement, and through achievement, the ability to experience psychological growth.

Figure 8.6 – Herzberg's hygiene and motivation factors

How do you distinguish between hygiene and motivator factors? Just ask your team two simple questions:

1. What makes you work?
2. What makes you work well?

Herzberg used the term "job enrichment" to describe how motivation factors can be used to achieve higher levels of satisfaction with a job. The following list was taken from his *Harvard Business Review* article of 1968 (reprinted in 1987), entitled "One More Time...How Do You Motivate Employees?" Take particular note of how closely these factors align with concepts embodied in self-direction. Meaningful job enrichment involves the following:

- Removing some controls while retaining accountability.
- Increasing the accountability of individuals for their work.
- Giving a person a complete natural unit of work.
- Granting additional authority to employees in their activity; job freedom.
- Making periodic reports directly available to the workers themselves rather than just to supervision.
- Introducing new and more difficult tasks not previously handled.

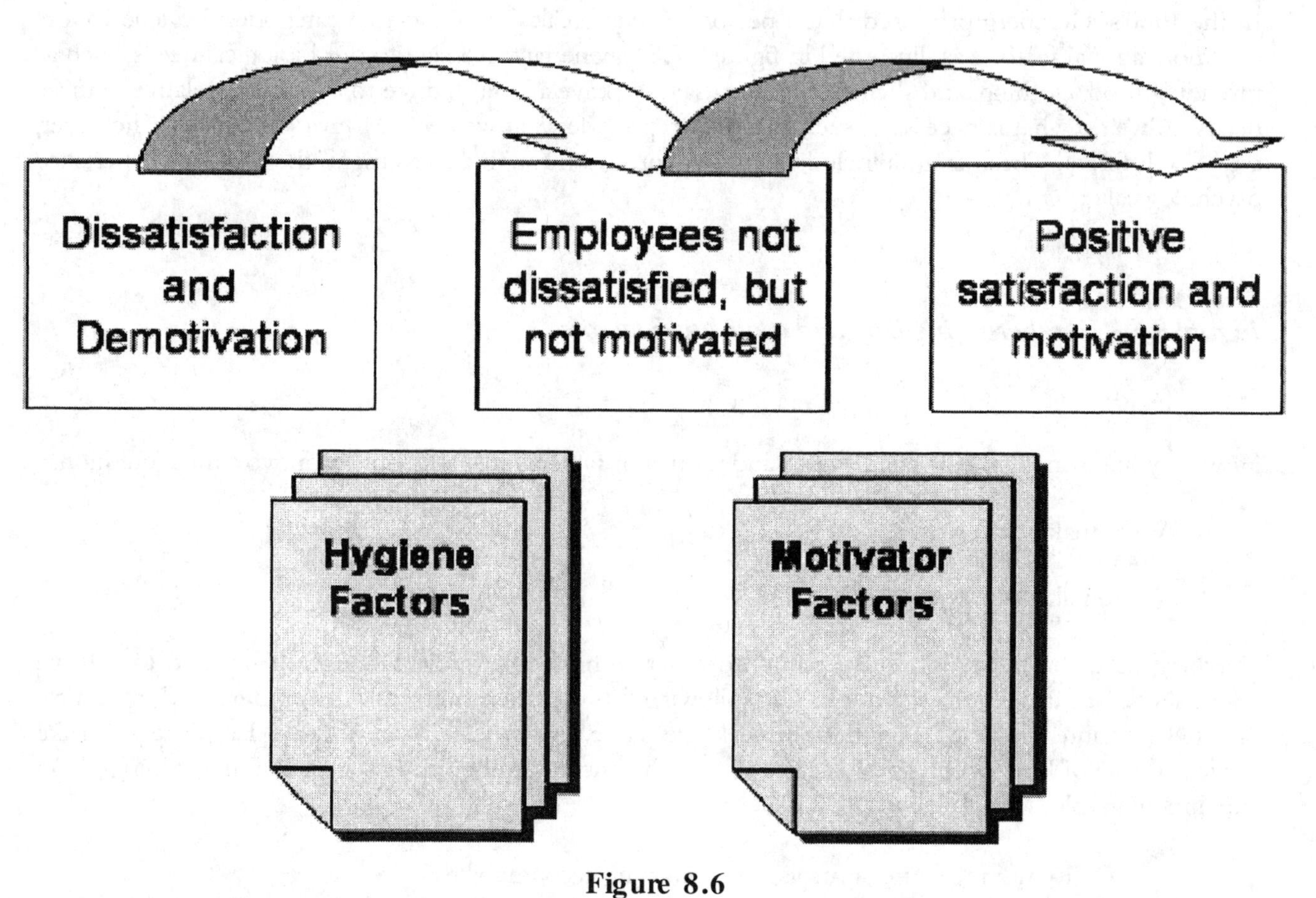
Dissatisfaction and Demotivation
Employees not dissatisfied, but not motivated
Positive satisfaction and motivation
Hygiene Factors
Motivator Factors

Figure 8.6

- Assigning individuals specific or specialized tasks, enabling them to become experts.

It is surprising to think that Herzberg first discussed these concepts in the 1960s, but that we began incorporating them in the 1990s. But self-direction will continue to grow because it makes sense in a highly competitive world. It also makes sense to a workforce desperately searching for dignity and meaning in its work.

Chapter 9 Building and Managing Virtual Teams

A flexible organization is competitive and responsive to the marketplace.

A virtual team leader is one of the many emergent professions of the knowledge and information age. New technologies dissolve the need to make space and time coincide, but they do impose, however, new rules and new conditions. This means that, respective to their degree of awareness, these professionals operate within working structures that require new means of organization and communication.

Distance project management becomes then both an opportunity and a challenge for them, and taking control of this factor requires both knowledge management and project management practice. This gives way to new continuing training needs to secure the professionalism, specialization, and retraining of e-team leaders, or e-leaders, and virtual team workers.

In informal surveys I have conducted with my project management graduate students at Boston University, as well as in my own practice, I have found that as much as 98 percent of project managers have not received any training on virtual project management, e-leadership, e-project organization, management of virtual teams or virtual project management office (ePMO).

However, while some professionals were not aware of ePM (or virtual project management), most of them were, and had actually been working in somewhat a mixed environment, not by choice, but by default, as a result of budget cuts, impossibilities of traveling or just plain workload. In any event, they all felt they could benefit from proper training in virtual planning, communication and human resources management, despite the fact they considered this type of training to be secondary. Most of them lacked the proper qualifications in these disciplines, and consequently acted rather intuitively. Besides, they argued, they do not have the time to learn more, and they have not found the proper material or the corresponding training offer.

This chapter attempts to provide answers for these needs and improve the qualifications of these professionals in the areas of virtual team (and project) building and management, quality management and control, and management and coaching of virtual teams.

Integrating Speed, Change and Radical Innovation

The role of a virtual team leader is neither a professional profile nor a new profession in itself. Instead, it is rather a complementary and intrinsic role of higher technical and managerial jobs within the new technologies' sector, because of the new work methods that these new types of tools provide and impose. In other words, it is not a profession strictly speaking, but a specificity belonging to the conventional project manager or team leader who saw the discipline evolving into a more ubiquitous, synchronous, and pervasive form, where the project manager had to deal with activities that were being developed on a distributed and delocalized basis through the use of new technologies, many already discussed in earlier chapters, or… not!

In order to be successful, virtual tem leaders and ePM managers must be able to integrate speed, change and radical innovation. Figure 9.1 illustrates a typical ePM environment.

Figure 9.1 – Typical ePM environment

Building and Managing Virtual Teams

When building the core task of managing a project, the efficient management of work being performed by the different virtual teams is a key factor to ensuring the quality of the final work. Individual local work and virtual teamwork should be homogeneous throughout project stages, and the final result should match the initial expectations.

Therefore, special attention should be given to the development of the virtual team. Responsibilities should be distributed according to the participants in the project, and their scope and level should vary according to:

- The importance and scope of the virtual teams, their purpose and the activities being performed.
- The degree of delegation and autonomy
- The virtual project workers in the remote project offices:
    - Work teams
    - Permanent or transitional collaborators
    - Local workers
- Their status within the project organization

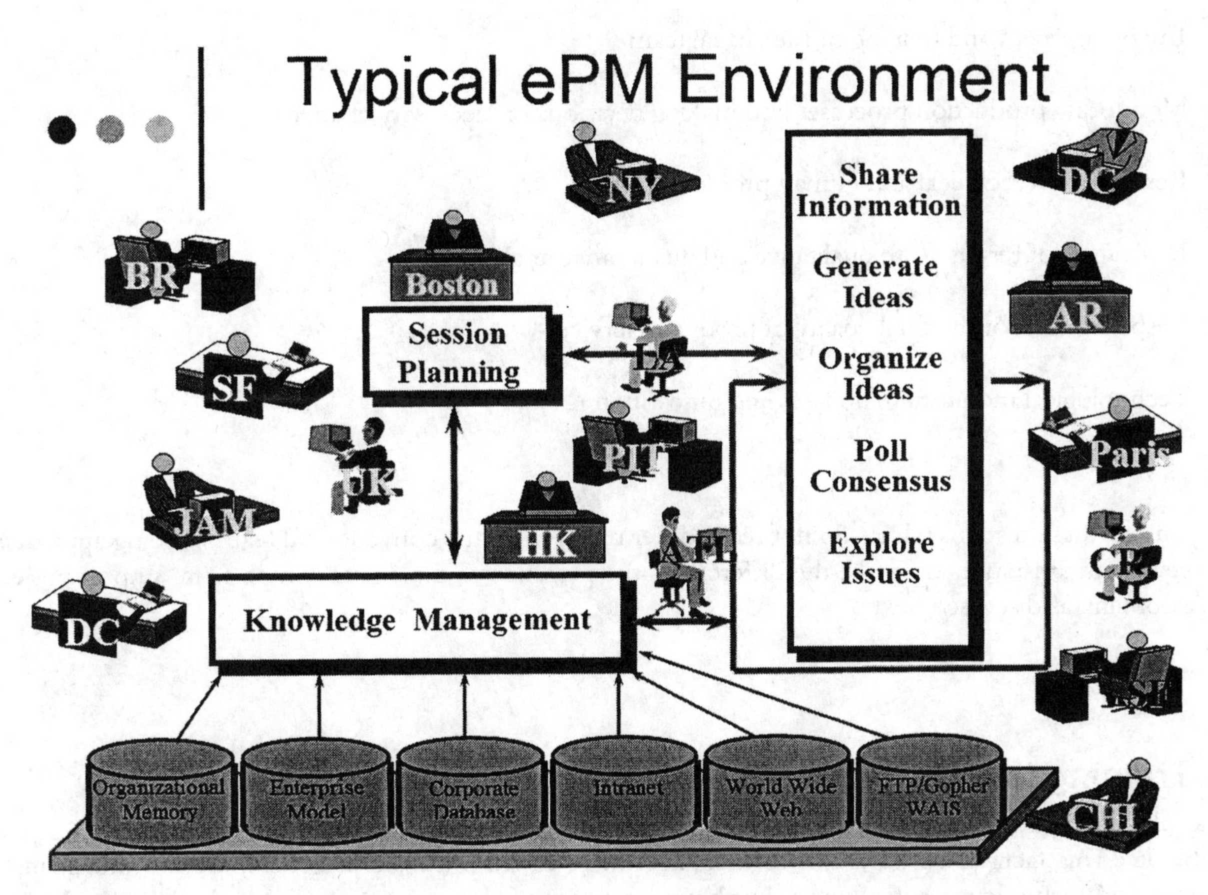
Typical ePM Environment
NY
DC
Share Information
Generate Ideas
Organize Ideas
Poll Consensus
Explore Issues
BR
Boston
AR
Session Planning
LA
SF
PJT
Paris
JK
JAM
HK
ATL
CR
DC
Knowledge Management
Organizational Memory
Enterprise Model
Corporate Database
Intranet
World Wide Web
FTP/Gopher WAIS
CHI

Figure 9.1

As for their responsibilities, they should pertain to:

- Development or participation in the initial design of products, services or projects
- Commercial relationships and contact with clients during the development of the product or project
- Design, set up and maintenance of virtual teams and remote project offices
- Organization and performance of work teams
- Coordination of work, tasks and actions
- Encouragement and training of the virtual team
- Monitoring production processes and making decisions on necessary changes
- Resolution of technical and human problems
- Evaluation of results from qualitative and quantitative analysis
- Responsibility for the final quality of products/services
- Technological monitoring/updates and innovation

As you see, these responsibilities do not really differ much from the conventional team-building approach. However, circumstances do make the difference - the presence of the digital component - impact project development, as discussed next.

Training is an Important Factor

One of the biggest caveats in virtual teams is that team leaders are not savvy on the technologies that enable it. This fact, however, is not to their detriment, as team leaders in general are not information systems and technology professionals. Furthermore, most of the literature available, both in books and magazine form, doesn't cover the subject. In a recent survey I conducted on the topic for another book I wrote[1], out of 60 virtual team professionals I interviewed, many were not familiar enough with technologies to help them manage their teams from afar. For the most part, these virtual team leaders were only familiar with e-mail, IM and Microsoft Project. Only three out of the 60 knew what Microsoft Project EPM was and of those, only one had worked with it.

Therefore, there is a tremendous need for training in the areas of virtual teams and virtual project management, especially on the technology side. Training professionals on these technologies is actually a

[1] Titled *Managing Virtual Projects*, by McGraw-Hill, 2005

great challenge due to the dramatic pace of technological innovation and the wide variety of tools and possibilities that can be available on the market.

Virtual team leaders, therefore, must keep up with the technological resources available, as this industry, I believe, is a never-ending flow of information and innovation. Specific training is being made available for professionals in large organizations, but there are very few training/consulting organizations focusing on training of ePM. I applaud the American Society of Mechanical Engineers (ASME) for the forethought in making such courses available as part of their curriculum. There is a course in virtual project management available throughout the year across the U.S.

How Virtual Teams Differ from Conventional Ones

When members of a virtual team congregate, either through technological means, such as intranets, extranets, Web Portals, instant messaging, phone conferences, etc., or through conventional means, such as getting on the plane and flying to the remote office, the responsibilities and tasks usually involve:

1. Participating in the design and set-up of the virtual workspace:

    - Analyzing the needs and requirements of the clients
    - Analyzing suppliers' offers
    - Preliminary assessment and evolution of the virtual project space, such as the Website, the discussion boards, and chats, together with the virtual team.

2. Organizing and securing the operation of the virtual project offices:

    - Setting up the organizational guidelines and the operational rules for end-users
    - Optimization of results in the work environment
    - Organization and management of the work schedule and activities
    - Management of economic resources related to the space
    - In some cases, performing administrative management tasks such as hiring, budgeting, invoicing, etc.

3. Coordinating the cooperation work, the actions and the activities related to the virtual project::

    - Defining the roles of the main participants in the virtual project teams
    - Establishing actions and exchanges pertaining to organization, operation, maintenance, coaching and training

- Organizing virtual (at a distance) or face-to-face project meetings
- Securing the monitoring and advancement of project work
- Defining and communicating commitments as necessary
- Evaluating the results of the actions engaged in the virtual project offices, and making the necessary changes in the virtual teams
- Acting as spokesperson with the clients
- Representing the work team before third parties

4. Securing project management and communications technology, maintenance and support:
   - Solving or participating in the solution of technical problems
   - Securing technological maintenance and innovation
5. Training and coaching
   - Training the virtual team members in communication tools such as e-mail, instant messaging, discussion boards, newsgroups, Microsoft Project EPM, and other project management tools.
   - Training the virtual team members so that they can effectively participate in the common virtual project workspace
   - Acting as mediator between the virtual staff, vendors, collaborators, partners, stakeholders, customer, etc.
   - Helping virtual project leaders to share the same values, criteria, and conditioning and orientation guidelines.
6. Evaluating the results:
   - Analyzing and summarizing actions and reactions from clients, stakeholders and project workers
   - Quantitative and qualitative analysis
   - Proposing solutions

There are also general tasks and functions that must be taken into consideration. In spite of the diversity of situations and activities performed by the whole virtual project team, the tasks and roles outlined below should be part of everyone's job description:

- Commercial relations
- Representation and public relations
- Consultancy and design of work
- Planning of tasks and activities
- Organization of work teams and the virtual workspaces where they meet:, design and set-up of operational procedures and guidelines
- Human resources management
- Technical and financial resources management
- Coordination and coaching of virtual teams
- Monitoring and controlling the state of advancement of the work
- Securing the quality of the processes and the results
- Providing technological support to the virtual team: orientation on the use of technologies and resolution of technical problems
- Securing innovation, mainly technological innovation

In the case of organizations where distribution and organization of teams was already set up to a great extent, you will find that the professionals who set up these teams were not typically the ones managing them. Several project staff exchange/share roles, act as virtual workers in some projects and as team coordinators in others.

Allotment of Working Time According to Functions

As for time allotment for the different virtual tasks assigned, it is typical to find the following main tasks performed by virtual teams, as depicted in figure 9.2:

- Business relations and communication with clients: up to 35% of the time.
- Project definition, planning and organization: 25%.
- Progress, performance measurement and quality control: 15%.
- Coordination and communication with virtual teams: 10%.

- Solving technical problems: 10%.

- Management of common virtual workplace: 5% (although this share increases in the case of those activities concerning Internet service providers and portals).

Figure 9.2 – Allotment of working time for virtual team workers according to functions

These data show that most of the time is devoted to communicating with the clients, although communicating with the virtual teams is also a very important task. Now notice how little time is devoted to revision of activities. It does not mean revisions are not important; as we all know, they are very important. But due to the nature of the working environment, virtual, a lot of time and thought is spent during the initial stages of the project.

As with my own projects, once I feel comfortable with the project leaders - that they understand the work that needs to be done, they are comfortable with their own teams, they know they can ask for help at any giving time, they are allowed to commit mistakes but should always take advantage of the communication technologies on hand and the vast technical resource available to them online and on the phone - once I know that, I just get out of the way!

Types of Virtual Teams

In the olden days of team management models, the motto used to be, "If in doubt, go travel to sort it out." However, this is highly inefficient and expensive, especially in a rapidly growing global organization. Many corporations are at the limit of what they can manage without huge structural changes, unless they develop a different way of working altogether.

I often find that senior executives are traveling twice as much now as they were two years ago (despite economic problems and the 9/11 impact). Many are already spending up to 6 weeks a year at 35,000 feet, not including the hassles of flying delays, taxis, hotels and jet lag. So what happens next year? The model of team management followed by most corporations is completely unsustainable and will become a number one survival issue.

Therefore virtual teams that can bridge the distance gap will win a clear competitive advantage, traveling less but with greater impact during each visit, backed up by regular videoconferencing, shared space technologies, chat, e-mail, telephone conference calls and other digital tools. And forget old-style video-links in boardrooms. Think wireless, everywhere, anytime, video-links that can start as spontaneously as a telephone call.

To achieve those results, however, you must understand the different types of virtual teams and their characteristics, so you can take full advantage of their potential. There are four types of virtual teams, as depicted in figure 9.3:

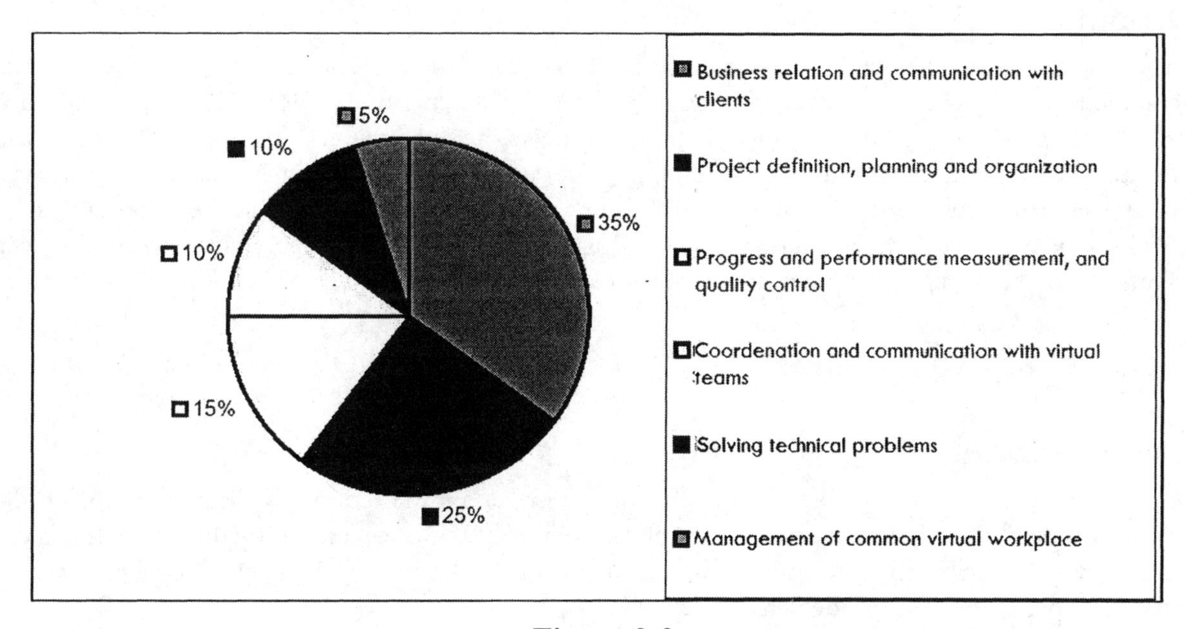
5%
10%
35%
10%
15%
25%
Business relation and communication with clients
Project definition, planning and organization
Progress and performance measurement, and quality control
Coordenation and communication with virtual teams
Solving technical problems
Management of common virtual workplace

Figure 9.2

- Local
- International
- Interactive
- Collaborative

Figure 9.3 – Types of virtual teams and time vs. place framework

Local

Local virtual teams are characterized as those that are located in the same world time zone and the same geographic location. The boundaries of what you call local will depend of your virtual team perspectives. A virtual team in Florida may be considered local, as it meets the two criteria -- same time and same place. In this case, we are considering same state as same place, while others may only consider same city, same town or even same building to be same place. In the case of having two teams in the same building, in order to consider it virtual, they either need to be physically separate or virtual in relation to another team. Of course, these distinctions are more semantic than anything else.

International

International teams are located abroad from the local team, in another country. These teams very often are more complex to work with, as cultures, local currency and languages tend to be different. In this case, when selecting a location for your international virtual team, make sure to develop an assessment matrix for site selection, as the example depicted in figure 9.4.

Figure 9.4 – Assessment matrix for virtual team site selection

Before establishing an international team and remote project office, you must understand your firm's competitive position in its global industry. Make sure to assess your firm's strengths, weaknesses, available resources and management's attitude toward implementing an international remote team. Questions you might want to ask yourself include:

- Why would you, or your sponsors, establish a virtual team abroad?
- Does your firm have adequate core competencies to sustain an alliance or merger project (language, cultural symmetry, political understanding, etc.)?

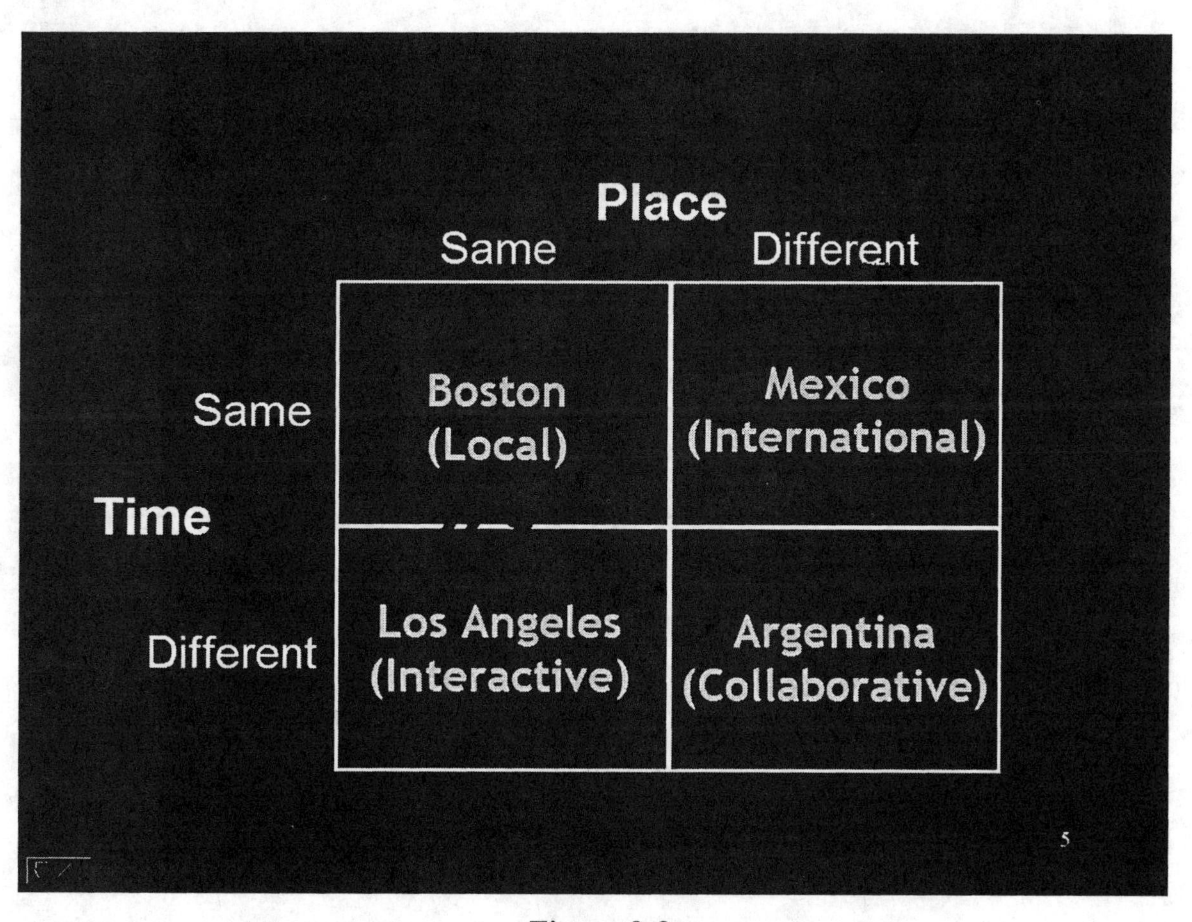

Place
Same
Different
Same
Boston
(Local)
Mexico
(International)
Time
Different
Los Angeles
(Interactive)
Argentina
(Collaborative)
5

Figure 9.3

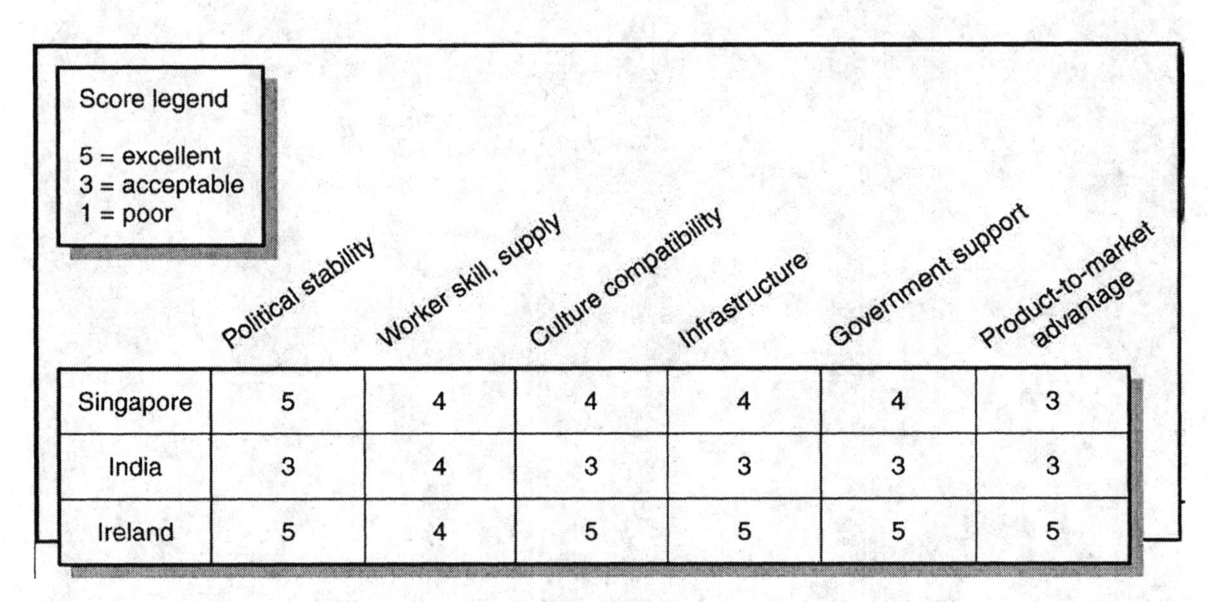

Score legend

5 = excellent
3 = acceptable
1 = poor

	Political stability	Worker skill, supply	Culture compatibility	Infrastructure	Government support	Product-to-market advantage
Singapore	5	4	4	4	4	3
India	3	4	3	3	3	3
Ireland	5	4	5	5	5	5

Figure 9.4

- Are you opening a remote office in light of competitive demand? If not, what's the reason?

- Do you have the financial resources available?

- Do you have multicultural exposure?

- Are you comfortable with the risk levels? I have been offered a couple of projects in Iraq, in which I would have to open a remote office there... No thanks!

There are many other situations you must consider, as outlined in figure 9.4, which include:

- **Legal/Political** – are you prepared to operate within the laws and regulations of the host country?

- **Security** – In some countries, the crime rate is much higher them you are accustomed to if you live in United States. The growing presence of organized crime has discouraged foreign firms from setting up operations in the former Soviet Union. In setting up projects in Angola, a common practice is to hire tribal bodyguards.

- **Geography** – This is an often-underestimated factor. I once provided consulting for the Institute of International Research in Dubai, in the United Arabic Emirates, and can tell you it was a shock to deplane at a brisk temperature of 105 degrees at 8:30a.m! The capital of Bolivia, La Paz, is in such a high altitude the most foreigners need a day or two to acclimate to the atmospheric pressure, which makes it difficult to breathe.

- **Economy** – How business is conducted in a country can impact your project. As mentioned earlier, this is one of the hurdles I have operating in South America, especially in Argentina.

- **Infrastructure** – Can the country provide you with the services requirements for your project? These include adequate transportation, communications, electricity, technology and educational system.

- **Culture** – Are you ready to accept and respect the customs, values, philosophies and social standards of the hosting country? Will religious factors impact the project? How about local languages?

Of course, the above is just a brief summary of issues you must consider when planning to set project operations overseas. It underscores the complexity of working on international projects, but I hope it gives you some idea on where to start if you have not been exposed to it. Great resources about every country can be found at the Central Intelligence Agency (US-CIA) web site at www.cia.gov, as well as the chambers of commerce of the cities in the countries you are contemplating. Also don't forget to check the Center for Disease Control (CDC) for health information at www.cdc.org.

Interactive

Interactive groups can be in the same locations or not too far from each other, with many similarities, such as language, culture, time zone, technology, background, etc., that allow them to establish a very interactive relationship. Distance does not necessarily prevent a virtual team's interactivity. For instance, you may have an interactive relationship between a team in the U.S. and another one in England.

Collaborative

Virtual team collaboration has captured the imagination of many professionals, with the purpose of enabling teamwork across distances, time and geographical zones. Boundaries between the team members of virtual teams are minimized by modes of electronic communication. By the nature of their distributed existence over the globe, virtual teams can be supported by Information Communication Technologies (ICTs), such as Blackboards or Web Boards that support chat, forum and other collaborative tools. In virtual teams, ICTs enable interaction between the participants and also impact on the team dynamics.

Technology is one of the aspects of virtual collaboration. A large variety of cultural and organizational issues also play crucial roles in the success or failure of virtual collaboration, as discussed extensively in earlier chapters.

Driving Forces behind Virtual Teams

There are several driving forces behind virtual teams, varying from technology and economics to competitive advantage and professional growth. Figure 9.5 outlines some of the main ones. But let's take a look at some of the other force in greater detail:

Figure 9.5 – Driving forces behind virtual teams

1. Virtual teams have more flexibility and adaptability than conventional teams:

- The ability to work together with virtual teams, instead of working in the same office or having to work overseas, offers flexible hours and the opportunity to work with professionals with whom you otherwise would not be able to collaborate.
- Virtual teams will be able to collaborate and communicate even after the project/product has been completed, as this type of communication does not rely on space and time; this contributes to that virtual team being able to work together again.
- Virtual teams can be set up to comprise many professionals whose lack of availability or mobility would not have otherwise allowed them to work together.

Driving Forces Behind Virtual Teams

- Conservative E-Commerce Project facts: (Source www.cutter.com)
  - 50% of new software projects are web-based
  - 20% of them are critical
  - 31% of IT budget spent of Web Projects
  - 95% should be done "within a year"
- Other Facts
  - Globalization
  - Downsizing/Rightsizing
  - Telecommuting
  - Partnerships and Alliances
  - Increasing Outsource trend
  - SWAT/Focused teams
  - Increasing competition, etc.

Figure 9.5

- Optimizing contacts between colleagues and collaborators
- Greater chances for innovation, since experts otherwise unavailable may be incorporated within virtual teams.

2. Better profitability of human, financial and technical resources:

- It enables the coordination of several projects to be executed simultaneously, without the need for too much traveling
- It enables the detection, preparation and management of projects with external collaborators in an easy way, improving project working skills and timeliness
- Project results can be delivered immediately via electronic means, and the feedback process can also start immediately
- Communication can be operative 24 hours a day, even with differing working hours and world time zones
- Once the initial technical investment has been made, general costs can be minimized (for instance, communication, trips, venues, infrastructures, etc.) on every scale
- It is easier to provide services to more clients without increasing production costs
- Time spent traveling and commuting decreases, and can be reallocated for project work or relaxation
- Flexible and autonomous management of working hours results in more satisfied virtual workers and a better quality standard in the working environment

3. Performance

- Better selection of professionals as they are not limited to the local market
- Easier and autonomous access to a wider variety of knowledge base, information and resources otherwise unavailable due to remoteness
- Technical support and solutions can be provided almost immediately
- Problems can be more easily spotted through automated software
- Communication standards accelerate and multiply without additional costs or strain
- Decisions can be made more easily considering the flow of information and feedback
- The distribution and allotment of tasks improves, as well as their monitoring and follow-up

- Information is automatically registered and made available as a sort of collective project memory

4. Improved professionalism

- The professional satisfaction and motivation of virtual tem members increases because they can participate more actively in the decision-making processes and can take on new responsibilities
- Virtual team members can work more autonomously, and make contributions and suggestions more easily
- Customer relations improve, especially for those overseas, as there are more ways of keeping them informed and participating in the project (in a very interactive fashion)
- Better planning and management of working hours
- Working hours become more flexible on a local and an international scale
- Virtual access technologies enable better organization and prioritization of urgencies
- Virtual presence helps save time and avoid unnecessary physical interferences and interruptions
- Time is saved when tasks are better coordinated in a global perspective

Dimensions of Virtual Teams

Virtual teams can be classified in four dimensions. While some scholars propose three dimensions, time, space, and culture, others identify people, links, and purpose as the strongest characteristics that distinguish a virtual team from a traditional team. There are other definitions, but I'd rather stick to one that is more business-oriented, as illustrated in figure 9.6:

- Stability of membership, which can be stable or fluid
- Clarity of team boundaries, which can be unclear or clear
- Timeframe in which to operate, which can be immediate or long term, and
- Regularity of activity, which can be regular or infrequent

Figure 9.6 illustrates typical characteristics among the dimensions

- Information is automatically registered and made available as a sort of collective project memory

4. Improved professionalism

- The professional satisfaction and motivation of virtual tem members increases because they can participate more actively in the decision-making processes and can take on new responsibilities
- Virtual team members can work more autonomously, and make contributions and suggestions more easily
- Customer relations improve, especially for those overseas, as there are more ways of keeping them informed and participating in the project (in a very interactive fashion)
- Better planning and management of working hours
- Working hours become more flexible on a local and an international scale
- Virtual access technologies enable better organization and prioritization of urgencies
- Virtual presence helps save time and avoid unnecessary physical interferences and interruptions
- Time is saved when tasks are better coordinated in a global perspective

Dimensions of Virtual Teams

Virtual teams can be classified in four dimensions. While some scholars propose three dimensions, time, space, and culture, others identify people, links, and purpose as the strongest characteristics that distinguish a virtual team from a traditional team. There are other definitions, but I'd rather stick to one that is more business-oriented, as illustrated in figure 9.6:

- Stability of membership, which can be stable or fluid
- Clarity of team boundaries, which can be unclear or clear
- Timeframe in which to operate, which can be immediate or long term, and
- Regularity of activity, which can be regular or infrequent

Figure 9.6 illustrates typical characteristics among the dimensions

Two Virtual Team Examples

	Project or Product Team	Action Team
Stability of Membership	Fluid	Stable/Fluid
Team Boundaries	Clear	Unclear
Timeframe	Longer-term	Immediate
Regularity	Frequent	Infrequent
Task	Non-routine	Non-routine
Decision Authority	High	Moderate
Complexity	High	Moderate

Figure 9.6

Another approach to the subject is to divide teams into subtypes and distinguish virtualness as a characteristic. In this context, there are four classes of team:

- Pure: team functions virtually, without control of any one organizational method
- Transitional: the team functions as a combination of hybrid and mono forms, and then one or the other
- Hybrid: the team functions in a multi-organizational culture
- The team members all function in the same organization

One gets the feeling that everything old is new again with the Internet. Perhaps there is truth in this statement, but recent technology has greatly enhanced the possibility of geographically dispersed employees working together on common projects. This thread of thought is weaved into related areas, such as corporate structure with virtual companies and virtual enterprises. Some concepts are taken from the older topic of telecommuting. Still others are from CASE tools that allow collaborative engineering. Most of the concepts from these ideas are shared, as is the literature.

Chapter 10
Team-Building Activities

Team activities allow group to recover from disunity, frustration and conflict.

Team-building activities are very important in any team-building process, not only in promoting teamwork, but also in demonstrating different aspects of team behavior and getting team members to think about what is essential to achieve high performance. These activities should be integrated in any team-building effort, as they allow the group to recover from disunity, frustration and conflict. They also help sensitize the team members to behaviors that may contribute toward or obstruct group problem solving. Behaviors cover such things as communication, problem solving skills, trust, taking advantage of the strengths and weaknesses of each team member, and understanding the customer's point of view.

This chapter provides a series of team-building activities for you to use in your team-building efforts. The exercises are just suggestions, just some examples to get you thinking. Every team has its own personality, likes and dislikes. Pick the exercises that make sense to you, feel free to innovate, to add to these exercises, and eventually come up with your own. There are lots of books and resources on the Internet. The important thing is for you to make this exercises are part of your team-building effort.

Get Off Your Chairs

Purpose: Team building, coordination, ice breaker.

Instruction: This is a great activity to get your team practicing quick coordination. This is a simple but fun and crazy relay exercise.

Instructions:

1. Use chairs or masking tape to mark a 5-foot wide, oval racetrack.

2. Form no more than four teams. Place a chair for each team at the starting line.

3. Each team will need its own color of inflated balloon and a paddle, such as a Ping-Pong paddle, a folder, or a magazine.

4. Have the first player from each team sit in their starting chair. Give each starter a paddle and an inflated balloon. (Have extra inflated balloons in case a team's balloon pops.)

5. Say: When I say, *"Off your chairs," first team members stand up and begin batting their balloon with their paddle around the racetrack. If your balloon hits the floor, you must return to your starting chair and begin again. You can hit another team's balloon once during the race. When you get back to the start, pass your paddle and balloon to the next person who's sitting in your team's chair. The first team to finish the relay wins. Ready? Off your chairs!"*

Star Light, Star Bright

Purpose: Team building, self-disclosure, great to use at the end of a team-building workshop.

Overview: This is a great activity to use at the end of a team-building session. Use it when you want people to think about <u>possibilities</u> rather than <u>impossibilities</u>.

Props: Cut out stars or you can use the one I provide here in Appendix A.

Instructions:

1. Ask team members if they have heard the rhyme, "Star light, star bright, first star I see tonight; I wish I may, I wish I might, have the wish I wish tonight."

2. Encourage participants to think of a wish that they have for the team, if their time together has shown them a glimmer of hope.

3. Pass out the stars and ask participants to stand in a circle. Explain that their sky is now the floor in front of them. Optional: Have participants place stars in a cluster on the wall.

4. Repeat the rhyme. When you finish, ask participants to come forward one at a time to place their stars in the circle on the floor and state their wishes.

Human Checkers

Purpose: Team building, self-steam builder, coordination, unity.

Overview: A huge checkers table results in a huge amount of teambuilding fun! Requires at least 26 players.

Instructions:

1. Tape alternating pieces of red and black construction paper in checkerboard-style in a large area.

2. There should be eight rows of eight squares. Each square area should be large enough for a person to sit on. Make sure the lower left corner of the "board" is black.

Appendix A: Star Light, Star Bright

3. Ask twenty-four people to be "checkers"—twelve black and twelve red. Have them each tape a square of red or black paper to their shoulder, according to their checker color. Tell them they can only move to black squares.

4. Choose two people who understand the game to be the players. Have them stand on chairs to see the overall board. Have them move their "checkers" following the rules of checkers.

5. To jump, the jumping checker must leapfrog over the other checker. When a player is eliminated, he or she must wait until needed to "crown" a teammate. Then he or she stands behind the checker that is crowned.

6. Continue until one team eliminates the other.

Famous People

Purpose: Allow team members to get to know each other, ice breaker, promotion of unity.

Overview: Use job applications to spark a guessing game of famous people.

Props: Blank enrollment applications and pencils. Get photocopies of your employment application.

Instructions:

1. Form pairs or trios and give each group one or two of the forms.

2. Have team member's work together to create fake applications based on popular fictional or historical characters.

3. Encourage members to have fun with "Previous Work Experience," "History Of Education" and other sections. For example, a form for Albert Einstein might list "the speed of light" as an area of expertise and "thinking up theories" as a hobby.

4. Have group members also put their names on their forms.

5. When the forms are complete, collect them and give each team a blank form to look at during the game.

6. Pull out a fake application, and then have one of the team members pick any portion of the form for you to read aloud (except the name, of course). See if team members can guess the character based only on the information in that portion.

7. Continue until one of the teams guesses the character.

8. Repeat this until teams have guessed the identities of all the characters listed on the forms (except their own, of course). The team that guesses the most characters wins.

Pipe Cleaners

Purpose: Exercise creativity, team building.

Overview: This activity allows participants to be creative.

Instructions:

1. At the beginning of the session (or during a break) place three pipe cleaners at each person's place.
2. Don't tell them what they are for unless asked.
3. When you are ready, tell the group they are to create pipe cleaner sculptures. In other words, they can do anything they want with them.
4. At the end of the session ask each group of five people to select a winner. Then have everyone select an overall winner.

If your culture encourages people to work in teams, make sure to give special recognition to any group that combines their pipe cleaners and uses all together to make something "better."

Knots

Purpose: Allow the team/group to recover from conflict (recover from figuratively getting all tangled up), disunity, and frustration. Also, this game works well if the group/team has just suffered significant internal dissention.

Overview: To get started with an icebreaker and form a group/team. This activity helps with team building and member's integration, as well as managing, observing, and experiencing individual preferences toward accomplishing a task. This is a good activity for supporting, coaching, influencing and encouraging positive behaviors.

Time: 8 - 20 Minutes

Participants: 8 – 20

Instructions:

1. Have the group stand in a tight circle with shoulders touching.
2. Everyone puts one hand in the center and takes one hand from someone across the circle.
3. Everyone puts their second hand in the center and takes someone else's hand across the circle
4. No one should be holding the hands of anyone next to them, or both hands of anyone else.
5. Explain task; "Untie the knots as far as you can."

6. Emphasize rule, "The hands may not break contact, though you may rotate your grip."

Managing the activity:

Occasionally two circles are formed. Sometimes the circle will break out separately and sometimes the two circles will be interlocked. If you wish to avoid this, pass a "squeezie" through the group at the very beginning, i.e., one person starts by squeezing the hand in their right hand. The receiver passes the squeeze to the next person, and so on. If the squeeze returns to the original person without touching everyone, there is more than one circle.

Occasionally you will have an overhand knot, which cannot be undone without breaking a pair of hands. It's often fruitful for a team to struggle with trying to undo an overhand knot.

When there are only 7 or 8 participants remaining, the leader should join the knot to provide adequate challenge. If the group is too small it won't work.. You need at least 8 people for this activity to be effective.

Broken Squares

Purpose: To develop team work, ice breaker.

Overview This exercise exposes the participants to behaviors that may contribute toward or obstruct group problem solving.

Time: 30 minutes

Participants: 6 - 18

Materials: A set of broken squares (pattern at the end of the exercise), Team Instructions, Observer Instructions.

Notes: Participation and cooperation by all members of a team are essential to attain team and individual goals. It is necessary to understand the objectives of the task at hand. Lack of communication makes the problem-solving process almost impossible. Problem solving requires that team members keep an open mind to a variety of potential solutions.

Preparation Instructions:

1. Make the broken squares by using the template in Appendix B.

2. Draw or enlarge on a copy machine, until each square is about 6 X 6 inches.

3. Cut the squares apart on the lines.

4. Mix them up and then put an equal (or about equal) number of pieces in 5 envelopes.

5. Make sure each group has 5 complete squares, or one set.

Appendix B: Broken Squares

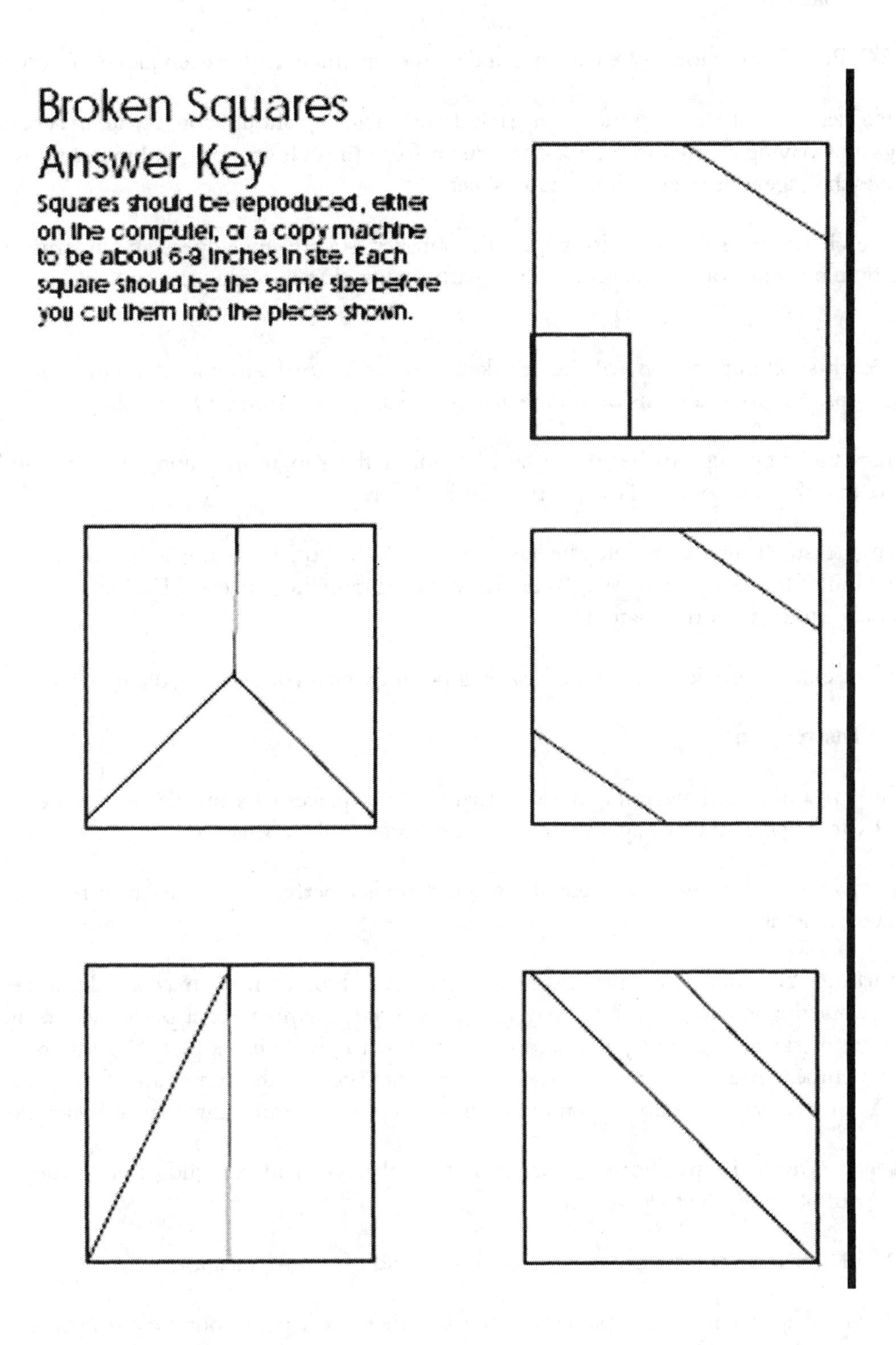

6. You will need one set for each team of 5 members. If you use card stock of 60 lbs. or heavier you should be able to use the same squares over and over again. (A good way to recycle old manila folders.)

7. Print Instructions for each team and a set of instructions for each judge/observer.

Note: Teams must have 5-6 members each. Each subgroup should congregate in separate locations. For subgroups having six members, ask one person from the sub-group to volunteer to as a judge/observer. Give each judge/observer an instruction sheet.

Give each of the subgroups its set of five broken square envelopes, and instruct the subgroups to distribute one envelope to each of the five participants. (Do not open the envelopes until instructed to do so.).

Give each subgroup its copy of the "Broken Squares Team Instruction." Read these instructions to the subgroups. Ask for questions or ask the group questions to ensure understanding.

Instruct the subgroups to begin the task.. Monitor the subgroups, along with the judge/observers, to ensure that the subgroups follow the rules fairly closely.

When the subgroups complete the task or time runs out, have the judge/observer help you lead a discussion of the experience. Ask, "What happened during the process?" Encourage the team to relate this experience to their work situation.

Have the entire team develop a set of learning points, which you record on a flipchart.

Team Instructions:

Each of you has been given an envelope that contains pieces of a puzzle. When the facilitator gives you the OK to begin, you may begin to reach your objective, which follows:

Objective: Your team will be successful when there is a perfect square, each of the same size, in front of each team member.

Important: You may use only the pieces provided. No member may speak or gesture in any way throughout the activity. Members may not ask another member for a piece, take a piece from another member, or signal in any way that another person is to give them a piece. Members may give pieces to other members. Members may not place their puzzle pieces in the center area for other team members to take. Your team will have up to 20 minutes in which to meet your individual and team goals.

Observer/Judge Instructions: Your job is part observer and part judge: As a Judge, make sure each participant observes the following rules:

1. There is no talking, pointing or any other kind of communication.

2. Participants may give pieces directly to other participants but may not take pieces from other members.

3. Participants may not place their pieces into the center for others to take.

4. It is okay for a member to give away all the pieces to their puzzle, even if they have already formed a square.

As an Observer, look for the following:

1. How willing were members to give away pieces of the puzzle? Were participants more interested in getting than in giving?
2. Did anyone finish their puzzle and then withdraw himself or herself from group problem solving? If so, how did it affect the rest of the team?
3. Did dominant individuals emerge, or did everyone seem to participate equally?
4. Did you detect evidence of frustration? How did it affect the group?
5. What was the critical turning point(s) affecting the teams working together?

Build a Car

Purpose: This activity helps teams to build identity and become more alert to the team's needs.

Overview: Break team into groups of four or five. Allow 20 minutes for the team to draw the car and 5 minutes for each team to present their vehicle. The total time depends on the number of groups you have.

Instructions:

1. Using flip chart paper, draw the outline of a car.
2. Instruct the group to add components to the car, and explain what each stands for and how they can relate that to the team.
3. Give one example and then let them go.

Some examples: Draw the antennae to make sure we have good communications or the wheels to keep us in motion. Others I've seen: the review mirror to keep an eye on where we have been, head lights to help us find our way, a trunk to store all our knowledge and tools, the gas tank to provide fuel when we need it, etc.

Glossary

Adjourning - The last stage of Team Building where the team disbands.

Administration - That part of the organization responsible for, or the act of, directing and managing the activities of the organization, program, project or major work package.

Administrative Change - A unilateral contract modification, in writing, that does not affect the substantive rights of the parties (e.g., a change in the paying office or the appropriation data).

Administrative Management - Management that operates in the public trust, such as national, regional or local government administrations. Designed to survive indefinitely, the intended goal is to provide an environment acceptable to its constituents for their survival, prosperity and comfort.

Assumptions - Statements taken for granted or truth.

Benefits Framework - An outline of the expected benefits of the program, the business operations affected and current and target performance measures.

Benefits Management - Combined with program management, Benefits Management is the process for planning, managing, delivering and measuring the program benefits.

Benefits Management Plan - Specifies who is responsible for achieving the benefits set out in the benefit profiles and how achievement of the benefits is to be measured, managed and monitored. The Benefits Management Plan is part of the program definition.

Brainstorming - The unstructured generation of ideas by a group of people.

Breakdown Structure - A hierarchical structure by which project elements are broken down, or decomposed. See also Organizational Breakdown Structure (OBS) and Work Breakdown Structure (WBS).

Conflict Management - The ability to manage conflict effectively.

Constraints - Applicable restrictions that will affect the scope of the project.

Contract - A mutually binding agreement in which the contractor is obligated to provide services or products and the buyer is obligated to provide payment for them. Contracts fall into three categories: fixed price, cost reimbursable or unit price.

Controlling Relationship - The early dates of an activity is controlled either by a target date on the activity or, more normally, by one of the predecessor relationships. In the latter case, the relationship is called the controlling relationship.

Coordinated Matrix - An organizational structure where the project leader reports to the functional manager and doesn't have authority over team members from other departments.

Corrective Action - Changes made to bring future project performance into the plan.

Delegating - The process by which authority and responsibility is distributed from Project Manager to subordinates.

Delphi Technique - A process where a consensus view is reached by consultation with experts. Often used as an estimating technique.

Dependencies - Dependencies are relationships between products or tasks. For example, one product may be made up of several other 'dependent' products or a task may not begin until a 'dependent' task is complete. See also logical relationship.

Dependency Links - Different types of links connecting activities in a precedence network.

Effort - The number of labor units necessary to complete the work. Effort is usually expressed in staff hours, staff days or staff weeks and should not be confused with duration.

Effort-Driven Activity - An effort-driven activity provides the option to determine activity duration through resource usage. The resource requiring the greatest time to complete the specified amount of work on the activity will determine its duration.

Effort Remaining - The estimate of effort remaining to complete an activity.

Engineering Cost Estimate - A detailed cost estimate of the work and related burdens, usually made by industrial engineering or price/cost estimating. Another term for Engineering Cost Estimate is Bottom-up Cost Estimate.

Exceptions - Those items that exceed the pre-defined acceptable cost and/or schedule variance.

Forming - The first stage of Team Building where members get to know each other and set up ground rules on behavior.

Functional Manager (FM) - The person responsible for the business and technical management of a functional group.

Functional Matrix - An organization type where the project has a team leader in each functional department and the products are passed from one team to the next.

Functional Organization - The hierarchical organization of a staff according to their specialty.

Gantt (Bar) Chart - A Gantt chart is a time-phased graphic display of activity durations. It is also referred to as a bar chart. Activities are listed with other tabular information on the left side with time intervals over the bars. Activity durations are shown in the form of horizontal bars.

Gantt, Henry - The inventor of the Gantt Chart.

Goal - A one-sentence definition of specifically what will be accomplished, while incorporating an event signifying completion.

Group - An assemblage of personnel organized to serve a specific purpose or accomplish a task. A group may vary from a single individual assigned part time, to several part-time individuals assigned from other organizations, to several individuals dedicated full-time.

Group Communication - The means by which the project manager conducts meetings, presentations, negotiations. and other activities necessary to convey the project's needs and concerns to the. project team and other groups.

Group Work - Work carried out in cooperation.

Groupthink - An undesirable condition in which all members of a group (e.g. a project team) begin to think alike or pretend to think alike. No members are then willing to raise objections or concerns about a project even though they are legitimate and based on hard data.

Implementation Review or Visit - An initial visit by members of the customer C/SCSC review team to a contractor's plant to review the contractor's plans for implementing C/SCSC on a new contract. Such visits should take place within 30 days after contract award.

Individual Work Plan - An individual work plan defines the responsibilities of an individual team member and is the lowest level of a technical plan.

Informal Review - A less formal subset of a quality review.

Leader - One who takes the lead or initiative through leadership.

Leadership - Getting others to follow direction.

Level of Effort (LOE) - Work that does not result in a final product (such as liaison, coordination, follow-up, or other support activities) and which cannot be effectively associated with a definable end product process result. Level of effort is measured only in terms of resources actually consumed within a given time period.

Line Manager - The manager of any group that makes a product or performs a service.

Management by Project - A term that is gaining popularity, used to describe normal management processes that are being project managed.

Management Development - All aspects of staff planning, recruitment, development, training and assessment.

Mission Statement - Brief summary, approximately one or two sentences, that sums up the background, purposes and benefits of the project.

Mitigation - Working to lesson risk by lowering its chances of occurring or by reducing its effect if it occurs.

Modern Project Management (MPM) - A term used to distinguish the difference between current broad range project management, which encompasses scope, cost time, quality and risk, from more traditional project management.

Motivation - The ability to stimulate, rouse, excite, galvanize, or innervate. Typically with a view to getting work done on time and within budget.

Motivators - The forces that induce individuals to perform; the factors that influence human behavior.

Motives - The drives, desires, needs, wishes, and similar forces that channel human behavior towards goals.

Negotiation - The art of achieving what you want from a transaction, leaving all other parties involved content that the relationship has gone well.

Norming - The third stage in team building where conflicts are largely settled and a group identity starts to emerge.

Objectives - Predetermined results toward which effort is directed.

Performing - team building stage where the emphasis is on the work currently being performed.

Performing Organization - The organizational unit responsible for the performance and management of resources to accomplish a task.

Program Management - The effective management of several individual but related projects in order to produce an overall system that works effectively.

Program Management Office - The office responsible for the business and technical management of a specific contract or program.

Project Boundary - The boundary of a project, which is defined to indicate how the project interacts both with other projects and non-project activity both in and outside of the organization.

Project Leadership - Leadership in the context of a project, e.g. leading with a focus on the project's goals and objectives and the effectiveness and efficiency of the process.

Project Management Institute - The American professional body for project managers.

Project Management Professional (PMP) - An individual certified by the Project Management Institute.

Project Manager - The person who heads up the project team and is assigned the authority and responsibility for conducting the project and meeting project objectives through project management.

Project Performance - The direct results of intended actions within the project setting.

Project Team Member - The people who report either directly or indirectly to the project manager.

Project Team Work - The forming of a group of people into a team that is to work together for the benefit of the project. It can be achieved in a formal manner by use of startup meetings, seminars, workshops, etc. and in an informal manner by getting the team to work well together. Motivating and resolving conflicts between individual members of the team are important elements of teamwork. Cultural characteristics of the team members should be given full consideration. Different cultures create different working needs.

Storming - The second stage of team building where conflicts arise as members of the group try to exert leadership and exert influence over methods of operation.

Team - A team is made up of two or more people working interdependently toward a common goal and a shared reward.

Team Building - The ability to gather the right people to join a project team and get them working together for the benefit of a project.

Team Decision Making - The process by which the project manager and his team determine feasible alternatives in the face of a technical, psychological, or political problem, and make a conscious selection of a course of action from among these available alternatives.

Team Development - Developing skills, as a group and individually, that enhance project performance.

Team Development Plan - A description of a training program for project team members for enhancing their skills both in the work required for the project as well as in working together as a project team.

Team Leader - Person responsible for managing a stage team.

Team Leadership - Leadership may be subdivided into Leadership Techniques i.e. methods used for motivation and Leadership Styles i.e. the manner in which the leader applies those methods.

Team Members - Individuals, reporting to the project manager, who are responsible for some aspect of the projects activities.

Bibliography

Adler, L. (2003) "The Importance of Team Building," *Business Mexico,* Vol. 13, No. 4 (April), p. 19.

Baldwin, M. D. (1998) "Innovative Team Building Practices for Professionals: Developing Inter-Group Skills to Enhance Effective Performance," *Innovative Higher Education,* Vol. 22, Iss. 4 (Summer), p. 291, 19p, 2 charts.

Barwick, J. T. (1990) "Team building: A faculty perspective," *Community College Review*, Vol. 17, Iss. 4 (Spring), p. 32, 7p., NAICS/Industry Codes 61121, Junior Colleges.

DuBrul, B. (1977) "How To Build Individual Performance: An Alternative To Team-Building," *Training & Development Journal*, Vol. 31, Iss. 3 (March), p. 3, 3p.

Goncalves, M. (2002), *The Knowledge Tornado: Bridging the Corporate Knowledge Gap*, Blackhall Publishing, Dublin.

Goncalves, M. (2005), *Managing Virtual Projects*, McGraw-Hill, New York.

Hartley, D. E. (2004) "OD Wired," *T+D*, Vol. 58, No. 8 (August), pp. 20-22.

Haynes, M. (2005) "Well-oiled Machinery," *PM Network,* Vol. 19, No. 3 (March), p. 60-62, 64-65.

Heintz, N. (2004) "Smells Like Team Spirit," *Inc.,* Vol. 26, No. 5 (May), p. 58.

Huszczo, G. E. (1990) "Training for Team Building," *Training & Development Journal*, Vol. 44, Iss. 2 (February), p.37, 7p.

Lederer, N. (1978) "Team Building," *Training & Development Journal*, Vol. 32, Iss. 2 (February), p. 34, 2p.

Levinson, M. H. (2003/2004) "The Truth About Managing People . . . and Nothing but the Truth," *Etc.*, Vol. 60, No. 4 (Winter), p. 441.

Mareso, P. A., et. al. (2005) "Ricardo Semler: Creating Organizational Change Through Employee Empowered Leadership," [computer file], *Academic Leadership,* Vol. 3, No. 2 (June/July/August)

Miller, B. W. & Phillip, R.C. (1986) "Team Building on a Deadline," *Training & Development Journal*, Vol. 40, Iss. 3 (March), p.54, 4p.

Nodar, J. (2005) "New Tampa port director faces team-building challenges," *Gulf Shipper,* Vol. 16, No. 9 (February 28) p. 59.

Newman, B. (1984) "Expediency as Benefactor: How Team Building Saves Time and Gets the Job Done," *Training & Development Journal*; Vol. 38, Iss. 2 (February) p. 26, 4p.

Owens, J. (1973) "Organizational Conflict and Team-Building," *Training & Development Journal*, Vol. 27, Iss. 8 (August), p. 32, 8p.

Palleschi, P. (1980) "The Hidden Barriers to Team Building," *Training & Development Journal*, Vol. 34, Iss. 7 (July), p. 14, 4p.

Pickard, J. (2004) "Team building," *People Management,* Vol. 9, part i.e.10, No. 17 (September 2) p. 40-41.

-- (2004) "Team Building Is No Picnic," *Employee Benefits* (April) p. 27-28.

Veersteeg, D. A. (2004) "My Most Important Leadership Lesson? Teamwork," *Principal Leadership* (Middle School Ed.) Vol. 4, No. 9 (May) p. 36.

White, G. (1988) "Managing Conflict / Organizational Transitions / Team Building / Organizational Development / The Technology Connection" (Book Review) *Journal of Occupational Psychology*, Vol. 61, Iss. 2 (June), p. 189, 5p.

Wigtil, J. V. (1978) "Team Building As a Consulting Intervention for Influencing Learning Environments," *Personnel & Guidance Journal*, Vol. 56, Iss. 7 (March), p. 412, 5p.